Radical Relationships

Make Love Come Alive!

Tom Zimmerman

Life Changers Press

Radical Relationships: Make Love Come Alive!

Copyright © 2013 by Tom Zimmerman
All rights reserved.

1st Edition.

Requests for information should be addressed to:
Life Changers Press
P.O. Box 13322
Scottsdale, AZ 85267-3322

Library of Congress Cataloging-in-Publication Data

Zimmerman, Tom
Radical Relationships: Make Love Come Alive! / Tom Zimmerman.

    p. cm.
ISBN-13: 978-0615925752
    1. Marriage —Religious aspects—Christianity.
    2. Interpersonal relations—Religious aspects—Christianity.
    3. Marriage counseling—Religious aspects—Christianity. 1. Title.

In the interests of privacy, some names have been changed.

All Scripture quotations, unless otherwise indicated, are taken from the Holy Bible, New International Version. © 1973.

All rights reserved. No part of this publication may be reproduced, stored in a retrieval system, or transmitted in any form or any means except for brief quotations in printed reviews, without the prior permission of the publisher.

Printed in the United States of America

Make Hope Come Alive!

This book is dedicated to:

Imperfect Couples—
You can grow a Radical Relationship!

∞

Barbara, my wife of 31 years—
What an encouragement to me!

∞

We love because He first loved us. − 1 John 4:19

Special Thanks

I have the opportunity to meet wonderful people every week. They share their lives, their challenges, and their dreams with me. I am privileged to help them on their journeys of life. I especially enjoy encouraging and guiding couples as they seek to build or rebuild their relationships. Much of the content in this book comes directly from the past 20 years of working with these couples. They have given valuable feedback about what works, what is a waste of time, and what I can do better to help them grow. I want to thank them for their openness and their perseverance.

I have learned even more about relationships through my own marriage. Thank you, Barbara, for loving me and helping us build a Radical Relationship of love, respect and kindness.

I also want to thank Amanda, Erika, Clark, Laurel and Barbara for their help on this project. These wonderful people read my manuscript, shared their thoughts, and helped shape it into its current form.

Table of Contents

Introduction 1
1   Radical Relationships 3
2   Radical Intimacy 11
3   Radical Life 21
4   Radical Faith 27
5   Radical Relating 33
6   Radical Responses 45
7   Radical Resolutions 55
8   Radical Release 67
9   Radical Respect 77
10   Radical Romance 87
11   Radical Vision 97
12   Radical Resources 109
13   Radical Service 121
14   Radical Parenting 129
15   Radical Rewards 139
Final Words 147
References 148
Appendix 1: The FourSteps of Peace 149
Walking In Wisdom Devotional Guide 151

How to Use this Book

This book may be different than you are accustomed to. It is intended to be part workbook, part inspirational, part motivational and, above all, challenging and practical. If I may I offer a few suggestions:

1. Write in this book. I've left plenty of room for you to jot notes, thoughts and questions, as well as to respond to the exercises.
2. Read each chapter twice, then complete the assignments before going on. Take your time to work through the book. Ideally, work through one chapter per week.
3. Do the Final Project assignment at the end of each chapter. If possible, share your thoughts with your partner and learn from one another.
4. Use the *Walking in Wisdom* devotional guide in Appendix 2 at the end of the book to stimulate your relationship with God. There is one page for each day of the month. Either read them together with your partner or by yourself.

About the Author

Dr. Tom Zimmerman has directed Life Changers Counseling and Coaching for the past 16 years. He has also been a pastor, missionary and campus worker. Tom and Barbara have been married 31 years, have 2 adult children and live in Arizona, where they enjoy camping, hiking and sailing.

To learn more about the author and Life Changers, please see the Life Changers website: www.azchristiancounseling.com. If you would like to share your story how *Radical Relationships!* has helped you, you may reach us at: help@azlifechangers.com.

Introduction

This book is about being radical—becoming a radical and living and loving in a radical way. Perhaps you wonder, why use the word radical? After all, the idea of being radical is pretty unpopular today.

Over the past twenty years, we have been confronted with many negative examples of radicalism. Our political system has been stymied by angry radicals who refuse to work together. We have witnessed senseless destruction at the hands of religious radicals. Radicals were behind the 9/11 terrorist attacks. In our thinking, being a radical is almost synonymous with terrorism.

However, being radical doesn't necessarily mean being a terrorist or an angry politician. To be radical simply means to be significantly different, to be unlike the norm.

Radical:
very different, departing from the usual, non-conforming

Being radical is a hot topic today. There are literally dozens of books published yearly which use radical in their titles: radical dieting, radical politics and even, I kid you not, radical housekeeping! Several Christian authors have used the theme of being radical to challenge believers to rethink their lives and to live radically and transformationally (Platt, 2010).

My intent is not to be radical for radical's sake nor is it to copy someone else's ideas; rather, I believe couples need to be radical to succeed. The greatest radical who ever lived was Jesus. Not only was Christ different in the First Century, but His radical life and teaching still challenge us today. Instead of hate, Jesus showed love. Instead of being self-righteous, He forgave; and, instead of conforming to cold-hearted religion, He taught how we can build loving relationships with God and with one another.

Many couples today have relationship problems because they are "normal" instead of radical. Instead of becoming radical like Jesus and following His path of generosity, love and forgiveness, they adopt society's pattern for couples: materialism, complacency, and selfishness.

In our 31 years of marriage, Barbara and I have faced many challenges. Some of these challenges threatened to drive us apart. At other times, we have been tempted to settle into mediocrity, to conform to society's expectations of "normal." Although we are far from perfect, I thank God for our growth and perseverance.

We don't really look like radicals on the outside. We waive no banners. We conduct no street rallies. Our radicalism is measured by our relationships, to generously love God, one another, and others. With His help, we try to live radically every day.

My hope is that you will join us in becoming a radical, like Jesus. As you and your partner grow a radical relationship of love, imagine how your life will be different: your faith will become stronger, your relationship more loving, your family more connected, and your vision clearer.

1 Radical Relationships

When it comes to succeeding in life, most success comes through better focus and determination. If you want to get ahead at your job, you show up every day and do your best for your company. If you

> *To be truly radical is to make hope possible, rather than despair convincing.* — **Raymond Williams**

want to build a nest egg for retirement, you learn to manage your money and make wise choices about saving and spending.

These lessons don't always come easily. Many of us have learned the hard way. Do you know anyone who hasn't made some financial mistakes, especially when they were young? It's almost a rite of passage to stumble a few times along the way and, ultimately, learn to be a bit smarter and more diligent.

Everyone wants a good relationship. They want to laugh together, have fun, raise kids, be romantic, and live in peace and prosperity. However, when it comes to success in relationships, we often don't apply the lessons we've learned elsewhere in life.

Too often, we assume "it will just happen." We romanticize romance. We take for granted the relationship with the person we love the most. We are easily distracted and assume what started off well will continue in the same trajectory, like a rocket headed off into space.

Couples in Crisis

The reality, however, is very different. Couples today face great challenges. Most relationships begin with fun and romance, but then slowly become burdened with misunderstandings, pain and frustration. When couples are hurting, they are tempted to give up. Today, more marriages fail than succeed.

Let me introduce you to Adam and Ashley, a fictitious couple representing the challenges of many couples I've met over the years. After 10 years of marriage and two children, Adam and Ashley are in crisis. Both are frustrated with their relationship. Ashley expects Adam to pay attention to all of the details in life that are important to her. "He doesn't listen to me," she says. Ashley feels unloved and is then quick to point out Adam's faults.

Adam loves his wife but feels quite disrespected, due to her lack of appreciation and her frequent complaints. "She is always so negative." The more Ashley confronts Adam with problems, the faster Adam withdraws and puts his focus on sports, work—anything else.

As Adam and Ashley place unrealistic expectations on one another and demand more from one another, they grow further and further apart.

Over the past 20 years, I've worked with hundreds of couples in marriage and relationship therapy. When I ask what the main problem is, many couples tell me about their communication problems. Others focus on their money issues, while yet others aren't really sure what their problem is; they "just don't get along."

These problems of communication, finances, lack of respect and feeling unloved are very common and are very real to couples. However, I believe the central issues lie deeper. We easily allow three unhealthy mindsets to invade our thinking which lead to unhealthy, unsuccessful relationships.

Unhealthy Expectations

Have you ever noticed how it is so easy to become angry with your partner? You are tempted to say things to him that you would never say to the clerk at Wal-Mart. This is partly because you have much higher expectations of your partner than of the clerk.

Each of us has high expectations of things that are important to us, such as living standards, what roles we will play in the relationship and what we expect from our partners. These expectations usually come from our past. We embrace the values and habits that our parents held dear.

While some of these expectations are valid, others are unrealistic and unhealthy. When they go unmet, we can be deeply wounded. From there it is easy to become angry, spewing out mean or abusive words at the very people we say we love the most!

Let's admit it. Don't we often expect too much from family members, especially our partners? It is so easy to fall into using double standards, expecting much from our partners, while excusing our own behaviors or shortcomings.

Unhealthy Priorities

You have probably heard the phrase, "be careful what you wish for?" Too often, we focus on the wrong things. We fall into the trap of getting too busy, buying too many things, running in too many directions, and, in the process, losing one another!

One of the first things a young baseball player is told is "keep your eye on the ball." You can't hit the ball or catch it unless you focus on it.

Couples often get distracted from their relationships. They take their eyes off the ball and strike out. Things and activities take priority over the relationships. Love and communication get crowded out by busy lifestyles. Couples forget that relationships take effort, time, and work.

Unhealthy Selfishness

It is our nature to concentrate on ourselves, to use an imaginary prism to interpret how all of life's events affect us personally. When we are overly self-focused, we spend too much time and effort judging what we personally are getting out of our relationship. Then, it is easy to question how committed our partners are to meeting our needs and wishes. This lack of trust leads to an unhealthy level of insecurity and selfishness.

Can you see how such relationships will suffer and fail when both partners focus primarily on themselves? A pastor I know says this is like having two ticks and no dog—both people sucking the life out of one another! Relationships can't thrive when they are characterized by selfishness.

Exercise 1
Review the 3 unhealthy mindsets above: expectations, priorities, and selfishness.

Which of these have you experienced growing up?

How do these affect your relationship now?

A Different Approach: Radical Relationships

Most of us know the key to abundant living is not found in focusing on ourselves and our needs or in trying to become like others. Rather, the happiest, most well-adjusted people are those who selflessly invest in others.

While we know this to be true, in general, it seems counter-intuitive to think about someone else when we ourselves are battling loneliness and insecurity. How can you give to others what you don't have?

God's solution for struggling relationships is to help us overcome ourselves and develop beautiful, healthy, loving relationships. Jesus said,

Give and it will be given to you. — **Luke 6:38**

The promise is clear—when you give your best to God and to the people He leads into your life, you will be blessed and provided for. This others-focused approach to life and love is precisely what couples need.

It should also be clear that you can't give what you don't have. If you want to generously give to your partner, you yourself need to "fill 'er up" with God's love. To love others effectively, you need to walk in God's love and experience His loving touch daily. Start by reading the Bible daily, using the Walking in Wisdom devotional guide in Appendix 2.

Do you agree with me that many relationships are unhealthy? Do you agree that you don't want your relationship to be like them? Then, maybe you'll also agree that building a relationship significantly different will be a good thing. In fact, it is vital to change how we do relationships.

This all sounds a bit radical, doesn't it? It doesn't fit with the norms of society. It may not be how you were raised. But, it works.

As we considered in the Introduction, to be radical is to be different, to not conform. If we choose to not conform to the typical patterns for couples, it is not with the goal of being different, but with goal of growing a wonderful relationship that thrives over the long-term.

How Relationships should be Radical

Radical relationships are different.

Rather than conforming to society's (worldly) values and expectations, radical relationships embrace Romans 12:2, which calls us to not be conformed to the world's patterns,

---

Do not conform to the pattern of this world, but be transformed by the renewing of your mind.

Following this, the goals and values of the marriage become fundamentally different. Your focus will be less on material things, entertainment and "fitting in." Instead, you and your partner will choose to live out common values that will lead you closer to one another, closer to God, and to be of service to others. Imagine how wonderful it will be to be freed from the pressures of materialism and conformity. Envision the joy you'll have with one another.

Radical relationships are God-filled and God-focused.

People who learn to walk with Jesus become more like Him, more loving and kind, less angry and judging, and more generous and peaceful. When couples allow God's Word and His values to impact their relationships in meaningful ways, they will demonstrate the fruit of the His Spirit in remarkable ways.

But the fruit of the Spirit is love, joy, peace, forbearance, kindness, goodness, faithfulness, gentleness and self-control.
— Galatians 5:22-23.

By growing and showing godly character in your relationship, you will create the environment for great things to happen in your midst: harmony, forgiveness, love, and joy.

Radical relationships are a blessing to both of you and to others.

As I mentioned above, Jesus calls us to generously give to others, believing that if we do, God will take care of us.

Perhaps you've heard about the woman in Atlanta who went to the law office of a family friend. She explained to the lawyer how painful her marriage had become. When the lawyer offered to draw up the divorce papers, she interrupted, saying, "I don't just want a divorce, I want revenge." At this, her lawyer responded, "If that's what you want, go home and start doing all of the things you know he likes. Make a special meal, be kind and loving and thank him for his hard work. Then, after two weeks of this treatment, pull the rug out from under him and demand a divorce."

A number of weeks passed and the lawyer hadn't heard from the woman, so he called her. "Are you ready for those divorce papers now?" "Oh no!" the lady responded. "The most amazing thing happened. I did just what you told me to do. I cooked for him, treated him well and thanked him for his work…and he reciprocated. He began loving and respecting me! We don't need a divorce because we now have a great relationship!"

Radical relationships are committed relationships.

Even though we live in a throw-away society where relationships are discarded as easily as a sandwich wrapper, our relationships can be different. Imagine the difference when a couple is committed to faithfulness, love, forgiveness and happiness. They don't hold grudges, give up, or settle for mediocrity in their relationship. When the hard times come, they persevere and learn to rebuild a relationship of harmony and joy. If they become stuck and don't know how to change, they find a coach to get them back on the path.

Dare to be Radical

When you and your partner begin a Radical Relationship, you will be challenged to rethink and restructure your relationship. Each of you will need to "buy in" to the concept of changing your goals and habits in marriage and follow Jesus' model of love instead of what society tells you. Then, you will learn biblical principles and practical skills to grow as people and as a couple.

Granted, this idea of changing how you build a relationship can be a little scary or overwhelming—but imagine the payoff—a loving relationship where you mutually give to one another and walk with God together.

Don't you want that kind of Radical Relationship with your partner? Then, let's get started on this amazing journey of love!

Chapter 1 Project – My Commitment

In the coming chapters, you'll learn how to grow and change, but the first step is to commit to the process. This commitment will help you both persevere and grow in trust as you work together.

__ I will do my best to grow and change in my relationship with my partner.

__ I will work through this book and apply what I learn, as best I can.

__ I will invite my partner to join me in this growth process.

__ I will ask God's help because I recognize we can't do it on our own.

2   Radical Intimacy

Now that we've started thinking about radical relationships, let's dig a little deeper by assessing where you are in your relationship.

I once attended a conference where the speaker shared from his experience as a diplomat in the Middle East. He often worked to promote peace between two neighboring countries in conflict.

> *I have decided to stick with love. Hate is too great a burden to bear.*
> —**Martin Luther King Jr.**

The diplomat explained how unlikely it would be for those nations to suddenly go from war to peace, from open hostility to being peaceful neighbors. They couldn't expect to achieve peace until they re-established the groundwork of communication and trust.

Expecting that would be like asking a blindfolded baseball player to swing at a 90 miles-per-hour fastball and hit a home run! It probably wouldn't happen.

Instead of swinging for the fences, there are several smaller, positive steps the parties could take to repair the broken relationship. To follow the baseball analogy, it is like getting to first base on a bunt single, to then be followed up with further singles, ultimately leading to winning the game.

Going from War to Peace

There are five phases in going from war to peace in a relationship:

CRISIS - CONFLICT - CO-EXIST - COOPERATE - COMMUNE

1. **Crisis**: This phase is characterized by hostility. The couple engages in frequent, intense fights or they are very disengaged, preparing to give up on the relationship.

2. **Conflict**: Most couples in conflict don't listen well. Each partner is intent on getting his or her point across, but doesn't understand what the other person is saying.

3. **Co-exist**: In this phase, the partners live alongside one another and get along superficially, but, they still aren't on the same page. Many couples spend most of their married lives in this phase.

4. **Cooperate**: At this point, both partners are working together and are happier. While the relationship is generally peaceful, one or both people may still be dissatisfied because they are missing the intimacy they long for.

5. **Commune**: To commune with your partner and establish a deep sense of community with the person you love is extremely satisfying. It is what most couples hope for, although many never reach this deeper level of intimacy.

When you want to heal and grow your relationship, think of **taking one step to the right**:

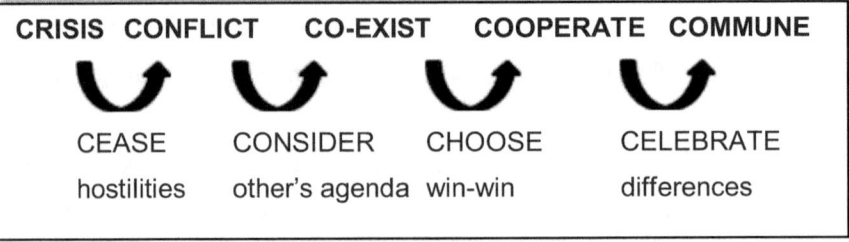

- If you are in crisis, work on stopping the immediate crisis, ceasing the open hostility. Agree to stop the destructive action of yelling, name-calling, blaming, and fault-finding.

- If you are in conflict, seek to co-exist with one another by listening to each other's concerns. Identify each person's agenda and identify your differences.

- If you are co-existing, seek cooperation and win-win situations. Agree to work together, choosing common ground and acting to further both of your interests.

- And, if you are currently cooperating, take the next step to community by building an intimate relationship where you commune with one another. Learn to celebrate the ways you each differ and celebrate your common interests.

Identify your partner's strengths and how they complement yours. Focus on the positives and give positive feedback to one another.

Exercise 1

Where are you and your partner in your relationship? Take a moment to think it over, then complete these sentences:

We are currently in the _____ phase. I feel this way because:_____

By taking a step to the right, we would reach the _____ phase.

In order to do this, we need to do the following better/differently: _____

I can help us move in this direction by: _____

When couples move away from War toward Peace by taking steps to right, they put themselves in a better place to thrive. They will be better positioned to grow intimacy in their relationship.

Challenges to Intimacy

In order to build relationships radically, we need to think outside of the box and act in ways that build healthy, lasting relationships, rather than what is typical in our society.

Most couples want intimacy, that deep sense of belonging to and caring for someone else. They want the passion and emotional bonds we associate with intimacy, but they end up frustrated. Let's look at some of the challenges that couples face.

Do you remember Adam and Ashley from Chapter 1? Ashley was frustrated that Adam didn't listen to her. Adam felt disrespected and avoided his wife. As time went on, they grew further and further apart. Their relationship digressed in phases, from cooperation and co-existence to the conflict and crisis phases.

When they first married, do you suppose they planned on a distant, C-minus relationship? Of course not! Just like all of us, they wanted an A-plus marriage, filled with love and intimacy and happiness. So, what happened?

External Pressures

Most couples start their relationship well. They have fun, develop common interests, talk for hours, and enjoy one another. Adam and Ashley started like this and assumed their relationship would continue to be good. Then, like many couples, they got busy and focused on jobs, kids, friends, finances, and all of the normal things that go into everyday life.

These everyday pressures work to split couples apart. It is as if you and your partner were each tied to raging bulls pulling you in opposite directions. Even if you dig in your heels, you will probably get pulled apart, resulting in distance and loneliness.

Internal Pressures

In addition to the issues pulling you apart, you also have issues inside your relationship that work to push you from one another.

Adam and Ashley hadn't always resolved their disagreements and irritations. Instead they swept them under the rug. They allowed little frustrations and misunderstandings to fester and build into big things.

Before they knew it, they had a mountain of issues pushing them apart from one another. Now, they not only had the external pressures of life pulling them apart, but they also faced the pain of internal strife.

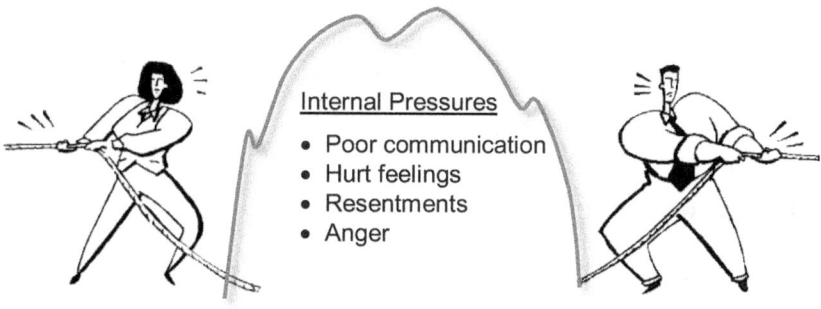

Internal Pressures
- Poor communication
- Hurt feelings
- Resentments
- Anger

If you purchased a new car tomorrow, I'm sure you would take care of this big investment by having the tires rotated and the oil changed regularly. You would probably change the oil every 3-7,000 miles because it is recommended.

Why wouldn't you save yourself time and money by only changing the oil every 50,000 miles? You wouldn't ignore the oil changes because that would be bad for the car. Can you imagine all of the dirt and grime that might clog up your engine?

I'm sure you are committed to maintaining what is important to you. However, Adam and Ashley took their relationship for granted and switched over to autopilot. Even though their relationship was important to them, they ignored the recommendations and didn't maintain their relationship well.

This led to the symptoms of poor communication, hurt feelings, resentment, and anger. In the midst of a busy family life, Adam and Ashley each felt misunderstood, hurt, and lonely. Instead of living in intimacy, they became roommates.

Exercise 2

Do you see how easy it is for couples to lose their intimacy? Write down the biggest challenges you think couples face:

What are the biggest challenges you and your partner face?

Radical Intimacy

Maybe you are wondering, "If it is so easy to lose intimacy, is there any hope for couples?" Of course there is hope! We can have hope and success because we will approach this idea of intimacy in a fundamentally different way. We will seek to learn and apply God's way of love and intimacy.

Stronger Stuff

We've looked at the challenges to intimacy, the external and internal pressures that try to push and pull you apart from one another. But there are powers available to you that are stronger than anything the world can throw against you.

The Apostle Paul tells us some important things about overcoming adversity. First, he reminds us that God is on our side and that He wants couples to succeed in loving one another,

> ***If God is for us, who can be against us?*** —**Romans 8:31 NIV**

Paul goes on to tell us what God's love is like:

> ***If God didn't hesitate to put everything on the line for us, embracing our condition and exposing Himself to the worst by sending His own Son, is there anything else He wouldn't gladly and freely do for us?*** —**Romans 8:32 The Message**

If that isn't enough, He reminds us again:

> ***Do you think anyone is going to be able to drive a wedge between us and Christ's love for us? I'm absolutely convinced that nothing…absolutely nothing can get between us and God's love because of the way that Jesus our Master has embraced us.*** —**Romans 8:38-39 The Message**

There is a fundamental principle to learn here. Relationships centered around God's love can do well. With God's help, you and your partner can have hope. You can overcome the stresses and pressures that want to kill your love and intimacy.

If you feel distant from your partner, perhaps one or both of you aren't as plugged into God's love as you need to be. Perhaps these Scriptures nudge you to seek Him and His love, and to share this hope with your partner.

When I look at God's Word, my perspective improves dramatically. I hope you have this experience also. Now, let's build on this hope more specifically.

Specifics of Intimacy

When I asked Adam and Ashley what they wanted in their relationship, they both said they wanted to be loved, accepted, and deeply connected with their partner. That sounds like most of us. It also echoes the basic concept of intimacy,

---

Intimacy—a close loving relationship with another person.

Remember the wild bulls that want to pull you from your partner and the mountain of hurt feelings that separate you from one another? Do you also remember the power of God's love that will help you overcome your challenges? Here is where we apply that.

There are three aspects of intimacy that you can strengthen to help you overcome the forces that want to separate you: spiritual, emotional and physical intimacy. They are like muscle groups which grow stronger if you exercise them, but turn to jello if you ignore them.

Connecting with your partner emotionally is central to everything people long for in a relationship—communicating on a deeper level, supporting one another, sharing the good times and the bad times together, and confiding in one another.

Emotional Intimacy

- Healthy Communication
- Sharing with One Another
- Supporting One Another
- Confiding in One Another

Successful couples take time for one another and time to connect emotionally. When they exercise this muscle group over the years, they overcome life's challenges and do well together.

How we treat each other on the emotional level almost always affects the physical relationship. If a couple is doing well emotionally, the physical part usually goes well; but, if there is significant conflict or emotional distance, the physical relationship usually suffers.

When we marry we expect physical intimacy, something to be shared with no one else—holding hands, tender touches and hugs, kisses, and passionate sex. This physical expression of love is truly God's gift to married couples. It is something that they can enjoy and that can strengthen their relationship. It helps couples overcome, come what may.

- Tender Touches
- Hugs and Kisses
- Passionate Sex

Physical Intimacy

Spiritual intimacy is something that many couples overlook. It is an opportunity to include God, our Maker, right in the midst of the relationship. I am amazed how many Christian couples attend church but rarely share about God or pray to God with one another!

- Praying Together
- Share Dreams and Values
- "On the Same Page"

Spiritual Intimacy

We'll deal with this in Chapter 4, but let me encourage you now to start praying with one another. If you want a healthy, loving relationship, you need God's help to turn things around. Join together for a few minutes each day and ask His help, guidance, and blessing.

Beyond reading the Bible and prayer, your spiritual intimacy can include your dreams and the values the two of you share. As you strengthen this aspect of your relationship, you'll feel you are more "on the same page" and more connected with one another.

Chapter 2 Project

Consider
Take a few moments and review what you've learned from Radical Intimacy:

Which "muscle group" of intimacy are you as a couple strongest in?

Which "muscle group" needs improvement?

What do you wish to be different?

How can you personally improve?

Turn these thoughts into a prayer, asking His help.

Discuss
If you are going through this book together, talk with one another for a few moments, taking turns. Be careful not to blame your partner or inflame the situation. Here are some questions you could discuss:

What are you learning?

What do you think is our biggest challenge to intimacy?

How do the Scriptures from Romans 8 (pg. 17) impact you?

What could you do to improve things this week?

3 Radical Life

In your pursuit of a radical relationship, remember that a healthy relationship depends on two relatively healthy people who are committed to one another. If you want a healthy relationship, you need to work on becoming healthy yourself.

> **There is no passion to be found playing small - in settling for a life that is less than the one you are capable of living.**
> — *Nelson Mandela*

Why does it take healthy people for a healthy relationship? Think about this for a moment. Spiritually or emotionally unhealthy people have difficulty loving and respecting others because they are wrapped up in their own pain. If you bring two people with lots of pain and baggage together, they will have a hard time becoming a happy, well-adjusted couple.

Does this mean only perfect people should get married? Of course not! I don't know any perfect people.

My point is this, many of us have baggage and emotional pain. We recognize how easy it is to become self-absorbed, leaving little love for our partners. In order to effectively love others, we need to deal with the stuff that holds us hostage so that we can experience the good life and love God has for us. Our challenge is to get healthy so we can love healthy.

The Radical Rabbi

Jesus spoke about this challenge:

The thief comes only to steal and kill and destroy; I came that they may have life, and have it abundantly.—**John 10:10 NAS**

He promised His followers radical, abundant life. But, what does that mean? This abundant life has two parts.

First, He offers eternal life with God to all who believe in Him (John 5:24). This is the essence of the gospel—God will forgive us sinners, if we repent of our sins, believe in His Son, and follow Him. This eternal life is an amazing gift He makes available to everyone! It is the ultimate reward for turning to God.

The other part of abundant life is that your life can be full right now. You don't have to die and go to heaven to experience the abundance of God's love.

As I was writing this, I paused and looked at some of the things hung on my office wall….pictures of sailboats, family photos, sailing trophies, more family photos… Then, I just had to stop for a moment. I was overcome with gratitude for my abundant life. It's not abundant because of possessions or accomplishments, like boats or trophies. It's abundant because I am blessed with loving family relationships and with faith in God. My life has not been perfect or easy, but it is truly rich and abundant.

Let's look at the same passage in a different translation:

A thief is only there to steal and kill and destroy. I came so they can have real and eternal life, more and better life than they ever dreamed of. **—John 5:24 The Message**

Is your life full and better than you ever dreamed of?

Obstacles to Abundant Life

There are several reasons why we fail to experience and live the abundant life Jesus promised.

- **We listen to "the thief."**
  In this passage, Jesus called Satan the thief who will steal from you, kill you, and destroy you. He will steal your joy and kill your family harmony. Also, in John 8:44, Christ called him a liar.

- It is as if there are two little people sitting on your shoulders. One is the Holy Spirit who whispers in your ear, helping you love God and others. On the other shoulder, you have the evil spirit who lies to you and tempts you to be unloving and selfish. Who are you going to listen to? Every hour of the day, you choose whom you listen to.

- **We make wrong choices (sin) and believe we can't change.**
  All of us sin and hurt others. The challenge is to stop the pattern and turn around. If you listen to that bad guy on your shoulder who accuses you, you'll be tempted to give up.

- **We lose focus and perspective.**
  When life gets busy, it is so easy to become distracted from what is really important. As we discussed in chapter two, when we lose focus, we tend to drift from one another.

  If you have been distracted, now would be a great time to re-focus on what is important. Begin by rekindling a close relationship with God. Listen to Him by reading 10 minutes a day in the Bible. Start an on-going conversation with Him. Let Him fill you with joy and peace again.

- **We carry pain from the past.**
  If you've ever been wounded by someone, you know that pain from the past can hang around and dominate the present. Like travelling with too many suitcases, those hurts and setbacks become burdensome. They slow you down and keep you from enjoying the great life God has for you.

  If you want a radical, healthy relationship, you need to deal with your past. Make a list of the things that still bother you. Talk with God about them and look to him for healing your wounds. Forgive the people who have hurt you and let go of the wrongs done to you. If necessary, find a trained counselor to help you process the issues and the pain. You'll be glad you learned to release the past so you are free to move ahead with your life and relationship.

Get Healthy

What do I mean by being healthy? Since you are made up of physical, emotional and spiritual components, you need to work toward health in all three areas.

I'm sure you understand, that if you neglect your physical health, you may not be able to enjoy a long-term relationship. You might not be around. If you hold on to emotional pain or issues, you'll be limited in your capacity to love others. And, if you have drifted from your spiritual connection to God, you won't be able to draw on His strength for your life and for your relationship.

Adam's and Ashley's problems as a couple were partly due to some unhealthy things in their personal lives. Adam's irritation with his wife was related to his unresolved anger with his dad. Whenever she criticized him, he heard his father pointing out his faults all over again.

After two babies and too many snacks, Ashley no longer felt good about her appearance. This, in turn, led her to feel somewhat depressed and alone. They had both come to a crossroads in life—either they would continue on in mediocrity and pain or they would take steps to get healthy.

The good news is that they changed, with God's help. Adam learned to deal with his relationship with his dad and the pain and anger he was carrying inside. This helped him become more patient with Ashley. Ashley started working out and eating healthier. She developed some outside friendships with other women and began to lighten up on her expectations of Adam.

Now that we've looked at the abundant life God wants us to have and the challenges we face, please use the Chapter 3 Project to apply these truths.

Chapter 3 Project

Consider
What challenges do you face that prevent you from living an abundant life?

Do you feel healthy physically? What would you like to change?

Do you feel healthy emotionally? What would you like to change?

Do you feel healthy spiritually? What would you like to change?

Pray
What is holding you back from becoming a great partner in your relationship?

Turn these thoughts into a prayer.

Discuss
If you are going through this book together, talk with one another for a few moments, taking turns. Be careful not to blame your partner or inflame the situation.

Questions to discuss:
What did you learn from this chapter?

What is your biggest challenge to experiencing abundant life?

What could you do to improve things this week?

4   Radical Faith

We've looked at how things go wrong with relationships. We've also seen how couples with good intentions drift from one another and settle into mediocre marriages.

Now, let's start making your relationship better by doing things differently. Let's overcome the

> *Faith is permitting ourselves to be seized by the things we do not see.*
> **—Martin Luther**

forces of normalcy by helping you and your partner connect on a deeper level. The best way to start is by building your relationship around knowing and serving God.

Knowing God

Maybe you are asking, "What does religion have to do with my relationship?"

It stands to reason that if God created relationships, He is the best One to advise us on how to conduct them. Therefore, learning what God has to say about life and relationships will help us succeed in life and love. By following the Scriptures, we are literally following the user's guide, given to us by God.

Beyond this, though, there is much more to be gained by knowing Him. God is not just something to learn about, He is Someone to know and love and enjoy.

He promised us throughout Scripture,

I will never leave you or forsake you.
Joshua 1:5, Deut.31:6-8, Hebrews 13:5

For thousands of years, believers have clung to the promise that in good times and in very difficult times, God will be there for them.

Can you imagine this? The God who created the Universe has promised to be with His people. He wants to know and love you and for you to know and love Him.

Just yesterday, I spoke with a businessman who felt empty and lost. His friends and family had abandoned him; he had bottomed out in life. It was a privilege to point him to the one person who will never leave him.

You can know Him as your Lord, Friend, Savior and Guide through personal faith in His Son, Jesus. If you are uncertain of your personal relationship with God, I encourage you to find out more about becoming His child. Through faith in Jesus Christ, you can become a Christian and begin walking with Him (see Appendix 1).

As you develop a deep, loving relationship with Christ, you will discover the new life of abundance, challenges and joy that we discussed in the previous chapter. Beyond your personal faith in God, however, He wants to impact every facet of your life, including your relationship with your partner.

The Three of You

How did your relationship start? Was it like most couples… talking, flirting, movie and dinner dates? From there, did you spend more time together talking and having fun?

How often did you pray together? Most couples, even Christian couples, don't think to include God in their relationship from the beginning. Most couples certainly don't make God the center of how they relate with one another.

What is so radical about including God in your relationship? It is radical because that's not how we generally do relationships. Amazingly, when it comes to romance, we often forget God, our Creator.

In the allegory, *The Screwtape Letters*, C.S. Lewis wrote it is not necessarily Satan's plan for Christians to hate God, rather he just wants us to forget God (Lewis, 1941). Too often, we carry on in our lives and relationships as if God isn't around.

Adam and Ashley finally admitted they had made a mess of things. When they got past blaming each other, they came to the point where they realized they couldn't do it on their own. They recognized they needed God, the Master of the Universe, to unite them and guide them. By declaring their dependency on Him, they reached a turning point in their lives, their family, and their marriage.

This new humility and spiritual openness led Adam and Ashley to a new type of love and acceptance in their relationship. By orienting their relationship around Him and learning about His love and forgiveness, they were able to be more loving and forgiving toward one another.

If you believe God is all-powerful and all-knowing, why would you not want His help? Wouldn't it be a pretty good idea to tap into the wisdom and power of God for your relationship?

When our two children were small, I would sometimes help them cross the street by holding one by my left hand and one by my right hand. Together, the three of us would safely get to our destination. Although I was in the middle, we were all three connected together, going in the same direction.

Imagine you and your partner walking together, with God in your middle. There are three of you in this relationship. Even though you can't see Him, the three of you are together, heading in the same direction. He keeps you safe from danger, He shows you where to go, and He unites you. What could be better for unity and intimacy?

Risks and Rewards

Growing a spiritual relationship together, with God, can involve a number of things: worshiping together, serving others together, sharing similar values and dreams, studying the Bible, talking together about God and life, and praying together. Each of these components of your faith will help strengthen your relationship with Him and with one another.

Before we move ahead with spiritual intimacy, you may be wondering about the risks involved. Many people avoid their partners because they are afraid. They are afraid of being disappointed again or afraid of being hurt emotionally or afraid of the past repeating itself.

These fears are valid. People do get hurt, partners disappoint us, the past does sometimes repeat. But, the alternative is to keep the walls up between you and your partner. Do you really want to spend the next years of your life in lonely cohabitation?

I once worked with a couple in conflict who decided their only alternative was to completely divide the house down the middle. They planned to totally avoid one another: one-half of the house was hers, the other half was his. They only had to share the kitchen, so they created a schedule of who could use it when!

Even after dividing the house and avoiding conflict, they were unhappy. Fortunately, we were able to get them on the path of a Radical Relationship. A side benefit—both could use the kitchen whenever they needed to!

I hope you will see it is worth the risk to invite your partner to a deeper relationship, to a radical one where you look to God together and ask His help. Even if your partner doesn't fully join you, won't you both be better off by talking to and listening to God?

Step of Faith

When I meet with couples for the first time, if they are people of faith, I usually ask them how often they pray with one another.

The results of my un-scientific poll of several hundred couples are revealing. Ninety-five percent of couples having marital or relationship problems don't pray regularly with one another. They don't take the time to jointly ask God's help. In essence, they forget they need His help and direction.

I then follow up this question by asking them another question. Would they be willing to invest three minutes per day in doing something that could significantly improve their relationship,? It would cost them a total of 21 minutes per week to make their marriage better.

Over 90% of couples are willing to try, so I then instruct them how to start praying with one another.

How about you? Would you invest three minutes per day to improve your marriage? Would you then follow that up with three minutes every day for a week? Will you take a step of faith with your partner and ask God's help daily? Jesus made us a promise, "For where two or three are gathered in my name, there I am in their midst." (Matthew 18:20)

The promise is that if you and your partner join together in prayer, God will hear your prayer and bless you in a special way. He will be with you.

Does that mean all of your problems will go away? Of course not, but you will be blessed and your relationship will likely improve. Naturally, if you pray for a healthy relationship, you also need to take steps to help it improve.

If your partner is unwilling or unready to pray with you, don't give up on your marriage. Pray on your own for your relationship and work at loving your partner with God's love.

Exercise 1

Consider
What did you learn from this chapter?

What are you motivated to do?

Discuss
If you are going through this book together, talk with one another for a few moments, taking turns. Be careful not to blame your partner or inflame the situation. Share your answers from the questions above.

Chapter 4 Project: "The Three of Us" Time

You have two options for growing together spiritually. If you haven't been praying together, do Option 1 below. If you already pray together, go on to Option 2.

Option 1: Pray Together

- Sit together when you can be undisturbed for a few minutes.

- Hold hands and ask one another what each of you would like to pray for. (Don't use this sharing time as an opportunity to criticize or make speeches, just share a brief request with your partner.)

- Either aloud or silently, have each of you pray, asking God for those requests and thanking Him for His help.

- Conclude with an "amen" and a hug.

- Make an appointment with one another for your prayer time tomorrow. Do this each day for the next week.

Option 2: Read the Bible Together

- Read a passage of Scripture together. To get started, I have included the devotional guide, *Walking in Wisdom*, in Appendix 2 at the end of this book. Read one section each day.

- Conclude your time together with prayer.

5 Radical Relating

The most common complaint I hear from couples is that they are frustrated with their communication. Whether they misunderstand one another or are too busy to effectively talk with one another, poor communication lies at the root of many relationship problems.

> *When the trust account is high, communication is easy, instant, and effective.* — **Stephen R. Covey**

No two people will ever become perfect communicators, but all of us can improve. In order to improve, though, we need a different approach, a radical way of relating that is different from the patterns most of us fall into.

The fundamental change we need to make is going from self-focused communication to being partner-focused communication. Instead of focusing on talking "at" and telling our partners something, we succeed in communication when we focus more on what our partners are saying. By listening better, we become better "understanders" and ultimately, better communicators.

Wipeout

Have you ever seen the TV show on ABC, "Wipeout?" In its five year run on television, hundreds of participants have run timed obstacle courses over water and mud.

Envision it with me; the participant is jumping over hurdles, avoiding swinging obstacles, and leaping to raised platforms. Does he make it? Will she win the prize? None of them get through without frequently wiping out, falling into the pool below, and wallowing in the mud, foam, or water.

As observers, we laugh at the thumps, spills, and wipeouts. That's the idea of the show, to entertain us, to make us secretly glad that we aren't the ones wiping out. At the same time, don't you feel for them? Don't you want to help them find their way past the obstacle?

When it comes to communication in relationships, most of us are like the participants in "Wipeout." We often don't see the communication obstacle coming before we wipeout. Before we know it, we are swimming in the pit, frustrated and confused about how we got there.

The Wipeouts

Let's look at five "wipeouts" couples typically fall into. Then, we'll look at five relating rules, how you can avoid the pits and recover from the wipeouts. Finally, in the next section, we'll review these rules and apply them to your relationship.

Wipeout #1: We talk too much and listen too little.

Have you ever been in a conversation with someone where the other person doesn't seem to be listening? Whether the other person interrupts you to say something, isn't paying attention or talks at the same time you are talking, it is highly frustrating. You may feel like the other person doesn't even care about you.

It is human nature to focus on and talk about yourself. Everyone does this. However, with couples, if both people are talking and neither is effectively listening, communication becomes self-focused and totally ineffective.

When we talk better than we listen, one or both of the people will be offended, which may lead to further problems. We have an old saying, "God gave us two ears and one mouth for a reason!" We need to talk a little less and listen a lot more.

In his well-known book, "The 7 Steps of Highly Effective People" (Covey, 1989), business coach Stephen Covey wrote of this in his Step 5, "Seek first to understand, then to be understood." Covey said,

> *Communication is the most important skill in life. You spend years learning how to read and write, and years learning how to speak. But what about listening? What training have you had that enables you to listen so you really, deeply understand another human being? Probably none, right?*

The skill of listening when paired with a significant effort to understand your partner is vital to your success as a couple. Relating Rule 1 says:

In order to understand my partner, I need to really listen.

How can you become a good listener? Start off with these important steps:

- **Prioritize**: Turn off the TV, ignore the cell phone. Show your partner is important to you by prioritizing what she has to say.

- **Eye contact**: Let your partner know you are listening by looking at her.

- **Stop talking**: Don't interrupt or "talk over" your partner. Let her finish before responding.

- **Body language**: Observe your partner, what does the body tell you?

- **Feedback**: Summarize what she is saying. Don't debate it, just send back what you are hearing and ask if you understood correctly.

Taking the time to truly understand is one of the most important ways you can show love. Beyond listening to the actual words, your goal is to understand what is important to your partner.

Wipeout #2: We think we read our partners' minds better than we do.

After a few years, people get lazy in their relationships. Rather than taking the time to talk things through, it is easy to fall into the pit of assumptions. You believe you either "know" what your partner is thinking or what he or she will think about a certain issue. You may also expect your partner to read your mind and get upset if she gets it wrong!

The reality is much different. We are terrible at mind-reading! After 31 years of marriage, I still don't know many things about my wife, Barbara. I don't know what she will order at the restaurant or what outfit she will wear tomorrow—and I certainly don't know what she is thinking at any given time.

If I start to assume I know what she thinks or wants, or if she assumes things about me, we will be set up for a big wipeout. Down into the pit of frustration and misunderstanding we will go!

Imagine if you come home from the store and your husband is standing in the kitchen with a frown on his face. It might be easy to think he is unhappy with you, so you ask, "what are you mad about now?"

Do you see the wipeout coming? Do you hear the assumption you made? You assumed he was upset with you; however, you hadn't taken the time to ask if this was true. Maybe he was frowning because he simply ate too much of last night's leftover pizza. It might have had nothing to do with you!

How could you have avoided the wipeout and kept both of you out of the pit? By asking a simple question or two:

Hey, Bill, are you o.k.?
Hi, honey, what's going on?
Is everything all right? Have I done something to upset you?

Any of these questions would work. When you don't know something, reach out to your partner and ask. Here's the rule to remember:

Relating Rule #2:

Don't make assumptions, instead ask questions to clarify.

By showing you want to understand and not just make assumptions, you will show that you respect and value your partner and your relationship.

Wipeout #3: We think we are right, so our partners must be wrong.

In our society, it is easy to treat a relationship like your iPod. You can turn it on or off. It's black or white. You can use it or lose it. However, that doesn't really work with relationships.

Would you agree with me that your relationship is not a competition? It is not about winning and losing. It is also not about always being right. Your relationship is about you and your partner loving and accepting one another.

Many couples fall into the habit of arguing over little things. One person needs to be right and the other person is proved wrong. Many of the things you may argue about are very unimportant. Some of these disagreements may be about things that have no clear-cut answers.

When couples argue and focus on being right, it often implies disrespect for the other person. You may disagree about an issue, but when you focus on being right at all costs, it may communicate that you don't care how your partner feels. This can lead your partner to feel you don't care about her.

When I was a boy growing up in Illinois, several other boys joined me at the vacant lot across the street to play whiffle ball. The oldest one, Max, chose the teams and set the rules for the game. Of course, Max's team always won. After a few days, some of the other boys stopped coming to play. They were the losers. They didn't want to lose any more so they moved on to play somewhere else.

Losers take their toys and go home. They stop playing the game and look for someplace more fun to hang out. If someone in a relationship is on the losing side most of the time, she will leave or "stop playing the game" because it is no fun to always be on the losing side.

Relating Rule #3: Avoid win-lose situations, choose win-win instead.

You can avoid the wipeouts of win-lose situations by listening to your partner and learning what is important to her. If you don't agree with her opinion, don't reject it out of hand; instead, say "I hadn't thought of it like that. My opinion is…. Let's keep talking about it." Allowing your partner to save face is more important than always being right.

Adam and Ashley would often argue. She would state her opinion and insist he agree and follow her wishes. Ashley had to win. What was Adam to do? Either he would give in to his wife, again, or they would get sucked into yet another confrontation. Usually, Adam got quiet and found an excuse to leave the room. He "took his toys and moved on."

As they began to change their relationship, winning became less important to Ashley. She came to recognize she had value as a person and didn't have to be right all of the time. Ashley became more secure in herself and lightened up on her husband.

At the same time, Adam realized it wasn't good to always capitulate. He could speak up about his opinion, even if it was different than this wife's. He learned to do so by being a bit more diplomatic. By letting her save face, he could be assertive without being aggressive.

Wipeout #4: We get facts and feelings mixed up.

When Barbara and I first moved to Arizona, she was a teacher at a small charter school for delinquents and other troubled students. At the end of each day, I would ask how her day went. This seemingly innocent question set us up for the next wipeout.

Barbara's day was usually difficult, due to the challenging students in her class. She was either frustrated, sad, overwhelmed, or upset. My quick reaction was to help her by giving unsolicited advice. This usually led to silence. Somehow, my great wisdom wasn't what she was looking for!

I remember once when we repeated this pattern three days in a row:

> T: *How was your day?*
> B: *It was hard. I'm really frustrated about…*
> T: *What if you did this…?*
> B: *(silence)*

Finally, on the third day she added:

B: *Why are you trying to fix me all of the time? Do you really think I'm that stupid that I haven't already thought of your suggestions?*

We wiped out and fell into the pit of confusing facts with feelings. We weren't communicating on the same level. Barbara was sharing her feelings with me, while I was trying to fix things (facts) for her. In essence, we were missing each other, leading to a wipeout.

Wipeouts: "Fixing Feelings" or "Listening to Facts"

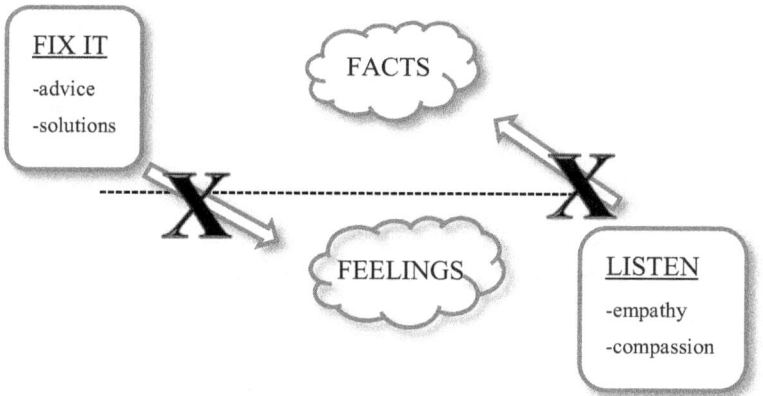

Here are examples of facts and feelings. Look for the differences:

Facts	Feelings
What time is our meeting?	*I'm upset about …*
We are out of milk. Can you please buy some?	*This is a great day. I'm so happy!*
What is our checking account balance?	*I'm sad because…*

Do you hear the differences in these sentences? When people are sharing or asking about facts, they want help and advice (fixing). When they share feelings, they want someone to listen to them and sympathize with them (listening). When we get on the wrong level of facts or feelings, we wipe out.

If you try to fix feelings, it usually doesn't work out well. Barbara didn't need my advice. She wanted someone to share her frustration and validate her. Instead, she felt misunderstood and judged.

Appropriate Responses:

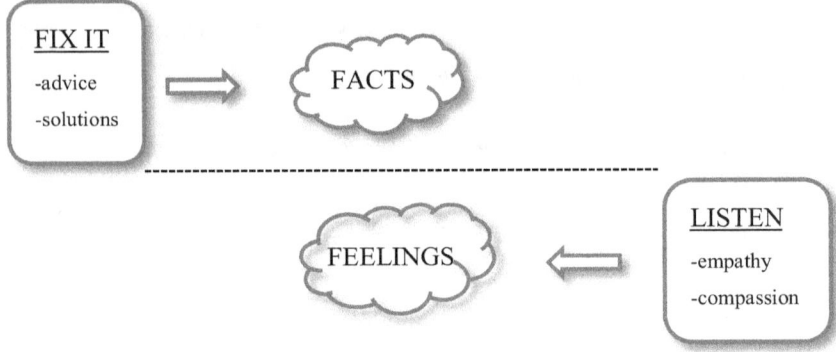

If you are talking facts and your partner responds on the feelings level, it can also be frustrating. Instead of getting help and assistance, you get sucked into a deeper conversation about how you feel. Here's the next rule to remember:

Radical Rule #4: Answer facts with facts (fix), answer feelings with feelings (listen).

How will you know when to fix it and when to listen? Listen to your partner. She will probably give you a clear hint. If you hear feelings, respond with listening. If you hear issues of facts needing fixing, respond with offers to help or with advice.

Exercise 1

Read the sentences below. Circle whether it is a "fact" or a "feeling", then give an appropriate response:

"I'm so frustrated."   Fact? Feeling?   I should respond by:

"She really upset me."   Fact? Feeling?   I should respond by:

"What time is the ball game?" Fact? Feeling?   I should respond by:

"I don't know what to do."   Fact? Feeling?   I should respond by:

Finally, if you're really not sure how to respond, ask your partner. "I want to help you, but I'm not sure if you would like my advice or if you just want me to listen...." Your partner will be glad you care enough to ask.

Wipeout #5: We give up too quickly.

A common pattern with couples is they give up too quickly on a conversation. If they don't immediately understand one another, it is tempting to either drop the topic or react too strongly to what has been said.

Remember the pit of assumptions we dealt with earlier? You don't intrinsically know what your partner is thinking, nor does he or she know your thoughts. In the same way, it is easy to misunderstand something that has been said and jump to the wrong conclusion.

You will never be able to perfectly understand one another. Misunderstandings happen with couples every day. If you don't clarify these hiccups with follow-up questions, you and your partner are likely to build a pattern of frustrating communication. It is tempting to get defensive, go on the offensive or throw up your hands and leave the room. To learn more about this, let's go back to Adam and Ashley.

It was a busy day. Before they left as a family for the church picnic, Ashley was overwhelmed with everything she needed to do: finish the egg salad, pack the picnic basket, load the car, and corral the kids. About that time, Adam came into the kitchen:

Ashley: *Adam, we've got to get ready. I need you to get the picnic basket and pack the car.*

Adam: *Oh, what's the rush?*

Ashley: *Don't you see everything I'm doing? We're going to be late and you aren't helping at all! Why can't you ever just do what I want? Aaahhh!*

Adam: *(silence, as he leaves the room)*

In Ephesians 4:26, Paul instructed us to deal with misunderstanding and hurt feelings right away.

Do not let the sun go down while you are still angry. (NIV)

If you take this command seriously, you will both choose to deal with misunderstandings and hurt feelings right away. You won't allow them to fester inside you and hinder your relationship.

This brings us to the last rule of relating:

Radical Rule #5: Go the extra step to understand your partner.

When you go the extra step to understand, you choose to ask follow up questions. If there is confusion, clarify it. If your feelings are hurt, talk it over. Don't allow disharmony or hurt feelings hang around. You can't afford it. Here are some examples of confusion and going the extra step:

He: *I don't have time for that right now.* (may lead to hurt feelings)

She: *Oh, is there something I can do to help you?* (she defuses, offers help)

She: *That really makes me mad.* (will he get defensive?)

He: *I'm sorry. What is the problem?* (clarify who/what she is upset at)

Can you see how investing two extra minutes can save hours of pain and frustration? Rather than allowing a misunderstanding to destroy your intimacy, you create an opportunity to build it.

It may take a bit of work to train yourself to respond differently. Intimacy grows not just in the good times, but also under adversity. By going the extra step, you can come alongside your partner and grow together.

Recap

Here is a summary of the Wipeouts and the Relating Rules we have covered:

Wipeouts	**Relating Rules**
#1 We talk too much and listen too little.	Listen more, talk less.
#2 We read one another's minds.	Ask questions to learn and clarify.
#3 We compete with one another.	Choose win/win: accept and support.
#4 We confuse facts with feelings.	Answer facts with facts, feelings with feelings.
#5 We give up too quickly.	Go the extra step: ask questions and clarify.

Exercise 2

Take a few moments and review what you've learned about Radical Relating.

What did you learn from this chapter?

Which "pit" are you prone to fall into?

What can you do differently?

Discuss
If you are going through this book together, talk with one another for a few moments, taking turns. Be careful not to blame your partner or inflame the situation. Share your answers from the questions above.

Chapter 5 Project: Couple Time

In addition to your daily "The Three of Us" prayer time from last chapter, your relationship needs time for communication. In the coming week, please spend 15 minutes daily talking together. Here are some suggestions:

- Choose a time free of distractions.
  (i.e. after the kids are in bed, turn off electronics)

- Touch and talk: sit close together, take turns talking and listening.

- Choose stress-free topics to get started. (i.e. Talk about how your day went, discuss something you both enjoy)

- Apply the "Rules of relating" you learned about in this chapter.

- Do your best to make it a pleasant, happy time

6   Radical Responses

Last chapter, we worked on changing your communication style from self-focused to partner-focused communication. By paying attention and really listening to your partner, you will understand one another better and lay the foundation for a stronger relationship.

In this chapter, we'll expand your partner-focused communication by helping you get better at responding to one another. We'll focus on three ways of responding to your partner.

> *The difference between the right word and the almost right word is the difference between lightning and the lightning bug.* — **Mark Twain**

Radical Responses

Ideally, you listen to your partner for a reason. You want to understand him and respond back in an appropriate way. By listening, understanding, and responding, the two of you can experience emotional intimacy and bond with one another.

How you respond to your partner's communication is just as important as listening to and understanding what has been said. Rather than responding to your partner in "normal" ways, we'll work on radical responses which are different and healthier. Your radical responses to your partner will help the two of you build trust, show respect, and improve the climate of your relationship.

Mirror, Mirror

Do you remember the "facts or feelings" wipeout we discussed in the last chapter? If someone is talking factually, he or she wants a response of advice or factual content. In contrast, if one person is speaking emotionally, the partner should respond by listening or supporting.

It is easy for couples to respond inappropriately when they misunderstand one another. Even when they hear what one another is saying, they may not really understand. That's why it's important to "mirror back" what you hear.

Mirroring, or active listening, is a simple skill in which you reflect back what you hear. Just like your bathroom mirror reflects back your image, so you can mirror communication by bouncing back what you hear your partner saying. You summarize the communication and send it back to your partner.

When you respond through mirroring, you will understand your partner better and be able to reassure him that you are paying attention. If your partner says he is tired tonight, you could respond with a quick fix, "Oh, then go to bed." However, unless you mirror back a response, you won't know whether your partner is physically tired or is discouraged. Instead, your response could be something like, "it sounds like you are tired, is everything okay?"

Think of playing a friendly game of catch with your partner. When he throws the ball to you, you catch it and throw it back. Here are some examples:

Message:	"I had a really tough day at work today."
Response:	"Sorry you had a tough day at work …would you like to tell me about it?"
Message:	"I don't know what I'm going to do with Jeremy."
Response:	"So you don't know what to do with Jeremy, is that right?"

Perhaps you have gone to sales training where you have been taught active listening. Too often, parroting back the words sounds canned or insincere. However, when you take the time to listen to your partner and reflect back what you are hearing, you employ a powerful way of connecting to him or her. Use your own words and style to make your response genuine.

You don't even have to agree with someone when you mirror back what you are hearing. You are simply actively communicating with your partner. By doing so, you will show you care enough to interact on an emotional level and that you and your partner are on the same team.

Let's continue on by looking at a second type of radical responses.

Warm Fuzzies or Cold Pricklies?

You may not often think about it, but when you receive a message from your partner, you have a choice about how you respond (Steiner, 1977).

When you respond in a warm, accepting, positive way (warm fuzzy), you communicate that you are eager to hear more, that you care about your partner, and that whatever he or she says is important to you.

A warm, fuzzy response is a response of love and acceptance, saying "I'm interested" or "I care." It helps you build up or restore your relationship. Warm fuzzies strengthen the relationship and make you both feel good.

In contrast, cold pricklies are rejection responses saying "go away" or "I don't like you." When you respond in a cold prickly way, you communicate rejection in that you don't agree, don't want to be bothered or are unhappy with your partner.

Do you give **warm fuzzies** or **cold pricklies**? Do you listen and respond warmly (restore) or do you ignore or reject the messages your partner is sending? How you respond to your partner will make a big difference in your relationship.

Exercise 1   Warm Fuzzy or Cold Prickly? Do I Restore Or Reject?

Read each scenario below, note what you believe the issues are, then make suggestions how the couple could have handled the response differently. (If you are reading this with your partner, have the man read the "he" part aloud, while the woman reads the "she" part.)

Scenario 1

He: *When I was telling you about the frustrations with my job, you told me to quit and go find a better one—that really bothered me!*

She: *All I could hear was you complaining. I thought you'd appreciate my advice. I'm only trying to be helpful.*

Analysis:
What is his issue? Why was he bothered?

Did she restore or reject his feelings?

Suggestions:

He was frustrated with his job and wanted some sympathy. Instead of supporting him, she "fixed it." rejecting his feelings. She could have let him vent for a while, then reminded him of her love and that she believed in him.

Scenario 2

She: *Last night when I mentioned my weight, I was so hurt that you were so judgmental; it made me cry.*

He: *You asked me if I thought you were overweight and I said, "Maybe a little." Don't you want to hear the truth?*

Analysis
What is her issue? Why was she hurt?

Did he restore or reject her feelings?

Suggestions:

Most women are sensitive about their weight! She wanted reassurance and he missed an opportunity to support her. Instead, he could have said, "You are beautiful and I love you."

Scenario 3

He: *I felt pretty humiliated when you told our friends how low my salary is. I wish you'd consult me before talking to others about our personal affairs.*

She: *Oh, sweetheart, I'm sorry. I guess maybe I'm still mad about how you spoke to my mother the other day.*

Analysis
What is his issue? Why was he upset?

Did she restore or reject his feelings?

Suggestions:

He felt violated that she had revealed a secret to outsiders. She got revenge on him for how he spoke to her mother. She should have brought up her resentments at another time.

Scenario 4

She: *When you wanted sex the other night, I felt like you weren't very concerned about me and what I was thinking about. We hadn't even talked very much that day. I feel like you aren't interested in listening to what I have to say!*

He: *Yeah, okay. We better get going now if we plan to make the 6:30 movie.*

Analysis
What is her issue? Why was she upset?

Did he restore or reject her feelings?

Suggestions:

She needed validation and to be taken seriously. He did neither. He needs to stop, listen to her, and prioritize her concerns.

To Speak or Not to Speak

Imagine going with your partner to a restaurant, placing your order and then waiting for a long time before your food arrived. By the time your meal is served, you are ravenous, almost ready to eat your napkin! Now, imagine digging into the food only to discover it is cold. That is, what was supposed to be hot is cold and what was supposed to be cold is somewhat cool.

What do you do? How will you respond? You have three choices in your response. Either you:

a. don't complain to the server, but grumble together about the cold food and agree to never come to this restaurant again. (Non-Assertive Response)

b. complain loudly and angrily to the server and the management. (Aggressive Response)

c. firmly but pleasantly explain to the server that the food is cold and request the situation be rectified. (Assertive Response)

Many of us have learned that we need to respectfully speak up for ourselves in restaurants, but many are not assertive when at home with the family. Instead, we either keep our frustrations and resentments to ourselves or we aggressively lash out at others when we are irritated or hurt.

Very often, people who have grown up with an aggressive parent overcompensate by drifting to the opposite end of the spectrum. They become non-assertive, holding their feelings inside and not speaking up about their legitimate concerns.

When one or both partners are non-assertive, the couple may have serious communication problems. This non-assertive pattern usually leads to bottled-up resentment and anger that will eventually come out. When it does, watch out! It won't be pretty.

People who are overly aggressive in voicing their feelings also have problems in relationships. If you have learned to get your way by being loud or angry, you actually may get what you think you want in the short-term. In the long-term, however, you will probably drive your partner away.

Ashley and Adam are good examples of being overly aggressive and non-assertive, respectively. Ashley was very vocal in complaining and demanding her husband's attention. If she didn't get what she wanted, she would raise her voice a few decibels and say the same thing again.

While Ashley was hanging out on the aggressive end of the spectrum, Adam took up residence on the non-assertive end. The more Ashley complained, the more Adam shut down and avoided talking about her issues or about the things he was concerned with. You can imagine how the level of frustration rose to the ceiling of their great room!

To overcome this problem, Ashley needed to work on being assertive, not aggressive. Adam needed to speak up assertively instead of shrinking away non-assertively.

Respectful Responses

Are Adam and Ashley the only couple with struggles in this area? Of course not! Many couples are challenged with being overly aggressive or holding their feelings inside.

How can they learn to respond differently? The Apostle Paul spoke directly to this issue:

God wants us to grow up, to know the whole truth and tell it in love—like Christ in everything. **Ephesians 4:15–The Message**

Healthy communication depends on honestly sharing your thoughts with your partner. God wants us to "speak the truth, in love." If you don't speak up (non-assertive), your partner won't know what you need or want. On the other hand, if you are overly aggressive when you speak up, your partner will likely withdraw and avoid you.

Instead, when you speak up truthfully, in a loving, respectful manner (assertiveness), you create the opportunity for healthy communication.

To overcome their problem, Ashley needed to work on being assertive, not aggressive. Adam needed to speak up assertively instead of shrinking away non-assertively.

Let's listen in as they learn to be assertive:

Old pattern
Ashley: *When are you **finally** going to help me in the garage?* (aggressive)
Adam: (silence, walks away)   (non-assertive)

New pattern
Ashley: *Adam, would you please help me in the garage?* (assertive, respectful)

Adam: *Sure, what do you need me to do?*   (respectful response)

Or, if Adam really can't help her right now:

Ashley: *Adam, could you please help me in the garage?* (assertive, respectful)

Adam: *Sure, I'll be glad to help when I finish
         with my phone call.*   (assertive response)

It's amazing how the communication climate changes when you radically respond with respect. Many of us aren't accustomed to assertiveness. We didn't grow up hearing healthy patterns of communication, but you can learn to become better at expressing yourself and responding to your partner. Try it out, you'll be glad you did!

In this chapter, we've worked on three types of radical responses. We first looked at mirroring, reflecting back what you hear from your partner. Then, we considered "warm fuzzies" and "cold pricklies," how we either restore and build up relationships or send messages of rejection. Finally, we addressed the issue of being assertive, as opposed to being aggressive or non-asssertive.

As you practice these three radical responses, I believe your communication will improve and the new levels of respect will dramatically impact the climate of your relationship.

Exercise 2

Take a few moments and review what you've learned from Radical Responses. What did you learn from this chapter?

What concerns do you have?

What are you motivated to do?

Chapter 6 Project

This week, please continue your daily 15 minutes of Couple Time. Here are some suggestions:

- Treat it like 15 minutes of fame! Prioritize your partner and your relationship. Sit on the same couch and talk. Turn off electronics, so you can focus on one another.

- Practice mirroring back what you hear your partner saying.

- Give plenty of "warm fuzzies;" limit the "cold pricklies."

- Go the extra step, ask an extra question. Invest 2 more minutes to understand.

- Be assertive, not aggressive.

- Remember to continue your "Three of Us" prayer time.

7   Radical Resolutions

I trust you have gained some valuable insights into rebuilding your relationship through these first six chapters. Now that we've laid a good foundation, let's build on your new communication skills by learning to deal with conflict in a radically healthy way.

> *People who fight fire with fire usually end up with ashes.*
> — **Dear Abby**

The Confusion about Conflict

In my counseling ministry, I meet many couples who have trouble with conflict. Either they avoid it at all costs, live in conflict as a way of life or are ineffective at resolving conflict. There are three areas of confusion about conflict.

Confusion #1:   If I avoid conflict, maybe it will go away.

Some people avoid conflict at all costs because they have had very painful confrontations in the past and don't want to repeat those experiences. They become conditionally trained to avoid conflict, believing that all conflict is necessarily painful. As a result, many people fear any type of disagreement and avoid resolving conflicts.

Realistically, disagreements and conflicts are inevitable in any relationship. People have different opinions and occasionally come into conflict with one another. If couples regularly avoid dealing with the conflicts that arise, the conflicts don't magically disappear; rather, resentments and hostilities develop.

Over time, such conflicted couples become distant and disengaged because they haven't dealt with the pain and disillusionment of the unresolved conflicts. In their desire to avoid the pain of conflict in the short-term, they set the stage for greater pain in the long-term as the mountain of resentment grows between them.

Confusion #2: I win! You lose! Life is good!

Some couples seem to thrive on conflict. They regularly "go to the mat" and argue over rather unimportant issues. It can easily become a competition to see who will win and who will lose this time.

Yesterday, as I was leaving my health club, I observed a father and his young daughter dealing with a conflict. The father was finished working out and came to the childcare area to pick up his little girl. She wasn't ready to leave her "friends," so the father chose the "win-lose" form of conflict resolution.

> *Megan, it's time to go home. COME!*
> *Nooo…don't wanna…sob, sob…*
> *I said COME NOW! (louder)*
> *Nooooooo! (louder still)*

By the time I was out the door, Daddy had slung Megan over his shoulder like a sack of potatoes while she continued her wailing. Daddy and Megan probably had a difficult ride home in the car.

When couples play "win-lose," they fail to recognize they are really playing "lose-lose." There are no winners, they both lose and the relationship loses.

Confusion #3: If we can't agree, we'll just compromise and move on.

What if someone gave you and your partner $100 for a romantic dinner at a nice restaurant? That would be pretty exciting for most couples!

On your way to dinner, imagine the two of you discuss where you would like to go. Your partner would like to eat steak but you really want sushi. After discussing this for some time, you can't seem to agree, so you decide to "compromise."

Let's compromise and go to McDonalds! You can order beef (hamburger, not steak), while I get the fish (-sticks, not sushi)!

How satisfied will you and your partner be? Even if you enjoy the time together, you won't be happy with the compromise. Too often, compromises are just another form of not resolving the issue. They don't satisfy either party.

Now that we've looked at the fallacies we often believe about conflict, let's find a better way of dealing with conflict by learning about radical resolutions.

Radical Resolutions

Let's begin by remembering the bigger goals for your relationship. You probably want a healthy relationship of harmony and teamwork, in which each person is valued and loved. This long-term commitment to succeeding as a couple means you need to resolve issues as they arise.

As we saw in Chapter 5, Ephesians 4:26 speaks to our need to resolve conflict:

Do not let the sun go down while you are still angry.

Couples can't afford to allow issues to go unresolved, leading to hostility and resentment. Instead, God tells us to resolve issues by addressing them daily.

Further, your goal in dealing with conflict shouldn't be for you personally to win an argument. Instead, your goal should be for you as a couple to win together. Let's call this "win-win," where each person feels heard, respected, and included. Even if you as an individual don't "get your way," it can be a win for you as a couple and, ultimately, for you personally as well.

What's so radical about resolving conflict and not having to win every argument? Envision that instead of conflict, resentment, and hostility, you and your partner learn to resolve issues and find "win-win" solutions you both feel good about. Instead of strife, you build and protect your harmony as a couple. That sounds pretty radical, much different from the norms of our society!

Building Consensus:
How to Resolve Conflicts, Confrontations, and Compromises

Adam and Ashley came to me with a big problem: they couldn't decide where to go on their summer vacation. He wanted to buy a used recreational vehicle and drive to Alaska. She was insistent they head to the beach in California.

Personally, it didn't seem like that large of a problem to me. Since they lived in central Arizona and they both wanted to escape the summertime heat, what's the problem? Anywhere is better in the summer than Phoenix!

However, it was a big deal to them, so we worked on their issue. When I asked them what they had considered doing before coming to me with their issue, they replied,

Adam and Ashley: *We've decided to compromise. Instead of Alaska or California, we think we'll go to Kansas!*

Perhaps you are scratching your head at this response like I did.

Tom (to myself): *Let's see: Kansas doesn't look like Alaska.*
Kansas has no beaches like California.
Why are they going to Kansas??

I never found out how they had decided on Kansas, except that it was a poor compromise like the situation earlier in this chapter about McDonald's instead of steak or sushi. I then suggested we find a better solution for them and explained how building consensus could help them resolve their conflict.

Consensus: an agreement, or harmony.

Consensus is a word we don't often use. When people work toward reaching consensus, they choose to do what is best for the common interest. It involves finding harmony and helps restore relationships.

Building consensus requires collaboration and cooperation. Sometimes, thinking creatively "outside of the box" helps people reach consensus with one another.

When I was a pastor in Vienna, Austria, our church made decisions through consensus, rather than by voting. We would identify the different concerns of people, discuss them at length, and continue discussing them until the church members were in agreement.

When you seek consensus as a couple, you sometimes may not reach complete agreement, but you can give consent to a solution that is acceptable or tolerable. "Is this proposal something I can live with?" On any given issue, something may be more important to your partner than to you, so you could offer to yield to your partner's wishes by giving consent.

There are two keys to remember in reaching consensus with your partner: flexibility and humility. The Apostle Paul addresses these keys in Philippians 2:3-4:

> ***Do nothing out of selfish ambition or vain conceit, but in humility consider others better than yourselves. Each of you should look not only to your own interests, but also to the interests of others.***

Humility is central to resolving conflict. If you remember that the world doesn't revolve around you and that other people also have important needs, you can create the opportunity to resolve your issues.

Humility is a function of your faith in God, your character, and your commitment to your relationship. When you trust Him to take care of your needs and when you pay attention to your partner's interests, you are well on your way to reaching consensus.

Consensus-building also requires both people to be flexible, open to new solutions, and considerate of the other person's concerns. If one person is inflexible and unwilling to consider other options, you won't be able to agree. However, by being flexible and open to creative ideas, you pave the way for "win-win" solutions that are good for both of you.

Creative Communication for Reaching Consensus:

When Adam and Ashley couldn't decide on their vacation destination, I showed them a simple format of asking five questions to build consensus and had them use the form on page 65 to record their answers to each question.

5 Questions to ask:

1. **Is this issue IMPORTANT? Is it important for us to agree on this?**

    There are many issues couples don't need to agree on, like when she goes shopping or what kind of tires he buys for the car. If the issue is unimportant, you would write "no" on the form and stop the discussion.

    However, other issues are very important to agree on. When Adam and Ashley planned to spend thousands of dollars on a summer vacation, it was important they come to a solid agreement they both felt good about. They wrote "yes" as their answer to Question 1 and then went on to Question 2.

2. **What is the ISSUE? What are we going to discuss right now?**

    It is important to identify what the specific issue is that you need to resolve; otherwise, it is tempting to drift between several different issues and you won't be able to resolve your differences. Simply write one sentence stating the issue, for example:

    "Where will we go on our summer vacation?"

    Then, go on to Question 3.

3. **What is the REAL CONCERN? What is the underlying concern?**

This step in the process is critical. Normally, when you disagree, it is tempting to state your own opinion over and over without really listening to what your partner is saying. At this point, it is important that you really listen to your partner. What is he or she saying? Why is this so important to her?

When I asked Adam why it was important to drive to Alaska, he responded,

It's hot in Arizona. I just want a break from the heat where I can be outdoors. I'd like to fish and camp and see some real trees.

Did you notice he didn't say anything about Alaska? That will be important to remember when we attempt to find solutions for this couple. We wrote his wishes down on the paper:

His concerns: **get a break from the heat, fish, camp**

Then, I asked Ashley why she was set on California. She replied,

When I was a little girl, my family always went to the beach in California. We had Mom, Dad and the kids together. We played in the water and made sandcastles...I want that same experience for my kids!

On the surface, it sounded like Ashley wanted to go to the beach, but the deeper concern was really about having family time together. I later learned it had been some time since they had had good times together as a family, so Ashley was determined that this summer they would re-connect as a family.

I recorded Ashley's concerns on the form:

Her concerns: **family time, beach, water**

If we stopped right here, Adam and Ashley would still be stuck in the disagreement phase where they would likely choose a poor compromise like going to Kansas. That's why it's important to invest a few more minutes and continue on by going to Question 4.

4. CREATIVE SOLUTIONS?
Brainstorm to find 5-10 possible solutions.

Now is the time to think outside of the box. Try not to fixate solely on your own position and remember to be flexible. What are possible solutions that may meet both of your concerns? Review the concerns both parties stated in Question 3 above.

When we reviewed Adam and Ashley's concerns, we suggested several possibilities, some of which had nothing to do with Alaska or California. That's because their deeper concerns weren't really about a specific destination, they were about him getting a break from the heat and her wanting significant family time.

If you aren't familiar with "brainstorming," it really is quite simple. As a couple, first state your concerns and wishes. Then, come up with possible solutions and record them. Don't reject or critique any of the ideas suggested.

When you think creatively and brainstorm together about ideas, it's amazing the solutions you may come across. Years ago, I needed to sell an old car I had been driving. I was willing to sell it cheap because it had a manual transmission. I found someone who wanted to buy it but she was hesitant to close the deal. When I asked why, she told me she had the money but couldn't drive a manual transmission car. Then we brainstormed and came up with a great solution: I would teach her to drive "a stick" if she would buy the car. After 15 minutes of instruction, she drove off in her new car!

After brainstorming, it is time to narrow down the ideas. It is usually pretty easy to eliminate several of the options and end up with the "top 3" best options. Keep talking and listening until you reach a solution you both can feel good about.

If you don't immediately find a solution you both agree on, don't give up. Put it aside for a few hours and then discuss it again, after prayer and reflection.

Exercise 1   Help Adam and Ashley Plan their Vacation

Please review "his concerns" and "her concerns" from Question 3 above; then, brainstorm together by coming up with 5-10 possible solutions. As you brainstorm, record the ideas below without critiquing or rejecting any of them.

What are Adam's concerns?

What are Ashley's concerns?

Possible solutions for Adam and Ashley

-
-
-
-
-
-
-
-

After you have listed the possibilities, narrow down the options to "Top 3" best solutions. Then, make a final choice what you think would be the best solution for Adam and Ashley.

Our solution for Adam and Ashley:

After listening to one another and after discussing the different options, Adam and Ashley reached consensus. They chose to split their vacation time between camping and fishing in the cool mountains of northern Arizona and some beach time in California. They were happy with their decision and enjoyed their vacation.

5. **RESOLVED? Is this issue resolved between us? Are we "on the same page?"**

The final question to ask is whether the issue is now resolved. Reaffirm your love for one another, touch, and pray together.

If you omit this crucial question, you may later wonder if the issue was resolved or not. By looking each other in the eye and stating your agreement, you will find peace together and you will grow in confidence in your ability to make good decisions as a couple.

Reaching consensus is about listening to one another, thinking outside the box and reaching "win-win" solutions. If you commit to the process of reaching consensus together, you'll find it is a powerful tool in helping you grow your radical relationship.

Exercise 2

Take a few moments and review what you've learned from Radical Resolution. What did you learn from this chapter?

What concerns do you have?

What are you motivated to do?

Chapter 7 Project:
Resolving Conflict, Finding Solutions

This week, use the "5 Questions for Consensus" to address and resolve an issue with your partner. With each question, share your thoughts and listen to one another. Remember to listen, be flexible, and be humble as you work together.

5 Questions to ask:

1. **Is this issue IMPORTANT? Is it important for us to agree on this?**

2. **What is the ISSUE? What are we going to discuss right now?**

3. **What is the REAL CONCERN? What is the underlying concern?**

My Concerns	My Partner's Concerns
-	-
-	-
-	-
-	-

4. **CREATIVE SOLUTIONS?**
   Brainstorm to find 5-10 possible solutions.

5. **RESOLVED? Is this issue resolved between us? Are we "on the same page?"**

8 Radical Release

Last chapter, we worked on resolving issues and preventing the pain that may otherwise occur. In this chapter, we'll work on what to do when you have hurt one another or let one another down. We'll focus on how to restore the relationship once damage has occurred. That's right, we'll be dealing with forgiveness, that act of restoration that is essential to every relationship.

> *Remember where we were kids playing ball. If we didn't get a hit, we'd stop the play and shout DO-OVER and we'd get to try it again?* —**Billy Crystal in the movie City Slickers**

Too Much Baggage?

When our children were small, we lived overseas and would visit our family in the United States every few years. On one trip, we brought all of the things we thought we might need, baby carseat, stroller, seven suitcases…it was literally a small mountain of baggage!

When we arrived at the airport, I went to the car rental desk to pick up the car I had reserved.

Tom: *Hello, I'm here to pick up my rental car.*

Agent: *Let me see…yes, here it is…we have an economy car for you.*

Tom: *Economy car? That sounds a bit small. Do you see those people and that mountain of stuff over there? That is my family and our belongings. Will all of that fit in your economy car?*

Agent: *Ohhh….it looks like you have too much baggage…*

Most couples have the dream of a happy home with healthy relationships. Too often, they don't reach their dreams because they are held back by excess baggage.

Just like my pile of baggage at the airport, they are encumbered by hurt feelings and wrong choices. It is too much for their relationships to handle. Either they continue to "schlep" these wounds and discouragements around or they must find a way to release the past and the pain.

Adam and Ashley had too much baggage. She nagged him, he ignored her. They both felt disrespected, resentful, angry, and hurt. They needed to get rid of their "stuff."

Radical Release

As we discussed in previous chapters, we shouldn't allow issues to go unresolved. If we "sweep them under the rug," we inevitably stumble over the issues and conflicts that divide us.

These unresolved issues also lead to pain. We let God down and hurt one another when we make wrong choices. The resulting wounds lead to scars and distance in our relationships. If this continues, the relationship degrades into dysfunction or despair.

Obviously, we need to free our relationships from the baggage and pain. We need a radical release from these burdens. What will free us up? How do we find release when we can't undo our histories of sin and failing one another?

Here is the great news! We can be freed, we can be released. God wants us to experience complete forgiveness from Him and with one another. Think of it as a two-pronged approach to forgiveness.

Forgiveness from God

The two-pronged forgiveness process begins with your relationship to God and then extends to forgiving others. Let's first look at how God forgives.

To describe God's forgiveness, Jesus once told of a servant who owed his king ten-thousand bags of gold. Talk about a big debt! I wonder if he was pre-approved for that mortgage!

The servant was unable to pay and begged for forbearance.

***Be patient with me,' he begged, 'and I will pay back everything.* —Matthew 18:26**

Obviously, the man would never be able to repay that large debt. Out of compassion, the master released the man from his debt.

***The servant's master took pity on him, canceled the debt and let him go*—Matthew 18:**27

Forgiveness means: to let it go, or, to release. Although we can't repay our debt, through faith in Christ, we can be set free. Out of His generosity, God is willing to forgive us.

The question arises, do we really have such great debts to God that could never be repaid? Are we really guilty? Have we been that bad?

The Bible teaches that, while God is perfect, we are very imperfect. He loves, we are selfish. He has high standards and expectations of us, how we should live, love, and think. Regretfully, we fall short. We'll never attain to His standard. We stand guilty before Him. Frankly, we are sinners.

Although we may already know this, we don't not like to admit that we are guilty. The selfishness, lies and cruelty in the world are evidence of our sinfulness. It is the norm and is part of the human condition. We fall short of what we could be and what God wants for us.

God wants us to know that we, too, can be forgiven. Like the servant who owed 10,000 bags of gold, He will release us from our debt. Thank God! Ask Him to forgive you by completing Part 1 of the Chapter 8 Project at the end of this chapter.

Forgive One Another

There is a direct connection between your sense of being forgiven by God and your ability to forgive others. If you want to forgive others, you need to experience being forgiven by God. Then, if you know God's forgiveness, extend that type of forgiveness to others. To expand on this, let's look at Colossians 3:13:

> ***Bear with each other and forgive whatever grievances you may have against one another. Forgive as the Lord forgave you.***

There are three commands in this verse:
- Bear with each other.
- Forgive one another.
- Forgive as the Lord forgave you.

The first command is to be forbearing with one another. Just yesterday, I discussed this subject with a young couple. They were bickering over little things and frequently finding fault with one another. Forbearance means to show restraint or tolerance with others, to not nitpick and find fault. Perhaps you are familiar with the old saying,

> ***If you point one finger at someone else, there are three pointing back at you.***

Richard Carlson, in his book "Don't Sweat the Small Stuff," reminds us that many things we fight over are pretty unimportant (Carlson, 1997). Couples can avoid many fights and hurts if they choose to lighten up with one another, to "bear with each other."

Instead of getting worked up with your partner about little things, loosen up a little. So what if he forgets to turn off a light or leaves something out of place. Isn't your relationship more important? Even if she is a few minutes late, does it really matter? Try out a little forbearance in your relationship. A little bit will go a long ways in improving the climate of your home.

The second command in Colossians 3:13 is to forgive one another. It doesn't say, "If you feel like forgiving, forgive one another." Rather, it is a simple command to forgive, to release someone from their debt to you.

To forgive: to release, to let something go.

When you choose to forgive and let it go, you are not choosing to release someone from their debt because they deserve forgiveness; rather, you choose to forgive because it is God's way and because it is the only way to heal the relationship.

The third command tells us the scope and nature of forgiveness.

Forgive as the Lord forgave you.

We are called to forgive with the type of forgiveness that God extends to us. Granted, we aren't God and we aren't as good at forgiving as He is, but He calls us to join in this forgiveness process anyway.

Why is this so important? Because forgiveness is essential to restoring relationships. Because forgiveness is good for us. Because forgiveness is God's way. Forgiveness is an essential part of loving someone.

If we want to forgive in the manner our Lord offers us forgiveness, it will be unconditional, complete and freely given. God is generous in forgiving people (us) who don't deserve forgiveness.

Do you know someone you need to forgive who doesn't deserve to be forgiven? None of us deserve forgiveness, but the generous act of forgiving anyway is an act of love and obedience.

Granted, forgiveness is hard work. It isn't easy for us. It wasn't easy for God, either. It cost Him His Son, Jesus. The impact, though, was amazing.

Through Christ, millions of people have been restored in their relationships with God. God's forgiveness literally changed my life. I trust your experience is similar.

Imagine the impact in your relationship when you choose to forgive your partner in the way God has forgiven you! Then, imagine how your relationship will be changed when you seek forgiveness from your partner. Angels in heaven will rejoice as the two of you are restored!

3 Steps to Seeking Forgiveness

Many of us know we need forgiveness and need to offer forgiveness, but we often don't get around to seeking it or offering it. To help you get started, think of three action words:

1. **Confess It: be honest, be specific, offer no excuses.**

    To confess it means to honestly admit the problem or mistake. You can't get started with forgiveness until you start talking about the issue.

    Be specific in what you did or failed to do. Don't make excuses for your behavior. "Man up" and own your mistakes. If you aren't specific or if you make excuses, you will disrupt the process and true forgiveness will be difficult.

    Start by saying something like this:

    "I did _____ and it was wrong."

2. **Express It: express sorrow, express commitment to change**

    When you express your sorrow, you recognize and admit that your behavior caused your partner pain. You can't undo the action, but you can share your regrets. Your partner may need to share how you hurt him or her. If so, listen closely and summarize aloud what you just heard.

    The other important thing to express is a clear commitment to changing your behavior. You need to share this so your partner can have hope for the future, that the hurting will stop. You can't guarantee that you'll never make another mistake, but you can share what you are planning to do differently so the future will be different than the past.

Now, the conversation might sound like this:

I did _____ and it was wrong. I'm very sorry that I hurt you.

Yes, you did hurt me. I can't believe you _____. It really hurt.

I acted wrong and hurt you. I feel badly for you. I want you to know I'm going to work hard to see this won't happen again. I plan to change this by doing _____ .

3. **Request It: "Would you please forgive me?"**

When confronted by one's mistakes, it is tempting to blurt out a quick "I'm sorry," and then end the conversation. People say they are sorry because they got caught or because the other person is upset. When you offer a quick "I'm sorry," you disrupt any chance to heal the relationship.

Instead, make a request by saying "would you please forgive me?" Those five words may very well be the most difficult words we ever have to say, but it is important to say them.

When you request forgiveness, instead of demanding it, you give the other person the choice of forgiving you. It is a sign of respect. Even though you didn't respect your partner when you made the initial mistake, now you are trying to reestablish respect in the relationship. You are saying, "I know you don't have to forgive me, but I would really appreciate it if you would."

Remember God's forgiveness. You don't get it by proving to Him that you are worthy, nor can you ever "make it up to Him." Rather, God tells us simply to confess our sins and request His forgiveness (1 John 1:9). In the same way, seek forgiveness with your partner by requesting it.

Here is how your forgiveness conversation might go:

I did _____ and it was wrong. I'm very sorry that I hurt you.

Yes, you did hurt me. I can't believe you _____. It really hurt.

I acted wrong and hurt you. I feel badly for you. I want you to know I'm going to work hard to see this won't happen again. I plan to change this by doing _____ .

I can't undo what I've done, but I would like to ask, "Would you please forgive me?"

Exercise 1

Take a few moments and review what you've learned from Radical Resolution.

    What did you learn from this chapter?

    What concerns do you have?

    What are you motivated to do?

Chapter 8 Project

Part 1 - Seek God's Forgiveness

Take some time to reflect on your relationship with God. Use this form to guide your thoughts and prayer.

Forgive as the Lord forgave you – Colossians 3:13

- **Confess It:** What do I need to confess to God?

- **Express It:** Tell God of your regret and your commitment to change:

- **Request It:** "Would you please forgive me for…?" (be specific)

Part 2 - Seek One Another's Forgiveness

Take some time to reflect on your relationship with your partner. Start by considering what you need to seek forgiveness for. Use this form to guide your thoughts and what you would like to say. Then, schedule a date to sit together and seek one another's forgiveness.

Forgive as the Lord forgave you – Colossians 3:13

- **Confess It:** What I need to confess to _____?

- **Express It:** Talk to _____ about your regret and your commitment to change:

- **Request It:** "Would you please forgive me for…?" (be specific)

9 Radical Respect

Much has been said and written in our culture about respect. Aretha Franklin sang about it. Pro athletes demand it. Parents try to teach it. We usually think of respect along the lines of the Golden Rule, to generally treat others as we want to be treated.

> *Consider the rights of others before your own feelings, and the feelings of others before your own rights.*
> —John Wooden,
> **UCLA Basketball Coach**

The problem with respect is, while we expect it for ourselves, we easily forget about it when dealing with others. Of course, it is human nature to be more concerned about ourselves than others. Society even seems to reward those who are more self-focused and demanding of attention.

Respect is linked closely with love and intimacy. To a great degree, the amount of respect in a relationship determines how far the couple will grow in intimacy. When we are respected, it paves the way for love to flourish. A lack of respect in a relationship can be devastating. Disrespect brings insecurity and pain, disrupting our intimacy with our partner.

What is so Radical about Respect?

It doesn't come naturally to truly respect others; rather, it is human nature to focus more on ourselves and our needs and less on our partner and his needs. The Apostle Paul pointed this out when he wrote about Timothy,

> *I have no one else like him, who will show genuine concern for your welfare…everyone looks out for their own interests.*
> **Philippians 2:20**

There aren't many people who are sincerely committed to serving and loving others. In the same chapter, Paul also challenged us to treat others like Jesus did, giving up all rights:

> ***In your relationships with one another, have the same mindset as Christ Jesus… Philippians 2:5***

We are called to think and act like Jesus, to care for others and lay it all on the line for them.

> ***Radical respect is a mindset, or intentional, thoughtful action. It means to consider others, to regard others' needs.***

Radical respect is also about making a choice—to choose to think about others' best interests over your own. Then, once you've made the choice to consider your partner's needs, you face the further choice of needing to give up your rights and prioritize the relationship with your partner.

Respecting your partner means saying to yourself, "I care so much about him that I will put his needs first." Showing respect communicates valuable messages to your partner which will enhance your intimacy.

To get a better grasp on radical respect, let's look at three ways you can show and communicate radical respect for one another.

Acceptance: "I Want You"

Perhaps the most fundamental form of respect is acceptance. When you accept your partner, you embrace him for who he is. Rather than focus on controlling him or changing him to your ideal, acceptance involves accepting him "warts and all."

True acceptance is not performance-based. You don't love and accept him because he makes lots of money or because he showers you with lavish gifts. In essence, you communicate to your partner, "I love you for being you!"

In contrast, the opposite of acceptance is rejection. It communicates "I don't like you" or "Go away" or "you aren't good enough." Most of us are very sensitive to rejection because we have been rejected by others in the past. It makes us feel insecure, unwanted, or unloved.

Needless to say, rejection hurts people deeply at the core of their being. When you reject your partner, it is like pulling an invisible trigger which reminds your partner of past pain from rejection. Even if you truly love your partner, your rejection messages may communicate the opposite to him.

When I meet with couples, a common form of rejection that comes up is pornography. Many men are tempted to view pornography. When they do and get caught by their wives, most men are embarrassed, admit it as a dumb decision, promise to stop, and want to move on. They often say,

It didn't mean anything to me. I love you. Let's move on.

However, most wives can't forgive so quickly because they feel personally and deeply rejected. Until they feel validated and accepted, they won't be able to move to forgiveness. They say,

I can't compete with those pictures.
I feel so inadequate. I'll never look like that.
What is wrong with me? Don't you love me?

In such situations, couples need to emulate God's type of acceptance. God accepts us unconditionally, regardless of performance or beauty. We are totally loved and accepted. When you lovingly accept your partner, you communicate God's form of unconditional love. Paul understood this when he wrote to the Romans,

Accept one another, then, just as Christ accepted you, in order to bring praise to God. **Romans 15:7**

Naturally, accepting your partner doesn't mean you necessarily accept or approve of all of your partner's behaviors. You are called to accept one another like God accepts you.

It pleases and honors God when you accept your partner as the person God made him to be. It is an on-going choice you make daily. There are many ways to demonstrate acceptance, including being affectionate, spending quality time together, being faithful and committed, as well as being careful to not reject or judge your partner.

Exercise 1   Am I accepted? Do I accept my partner?

Please complete this sentence: Recently, my biggest challenge has been: _____.

Please complete this table:

In this challenge I feel my partner…	completely	partially	not really
Respects me:			
Understands me:			
Accepts me:			
Supports me:			

Ask your partner to fill out this next part:

Please complete this table:

In this challenge I feel my partner…	completely	partially	not really
Respects me:			
Understands me:			
Accepts me:			
Supports me:			

Appreciation: "I value you"

Every culture in the world has a way of expressing thanks and appreciation. In my travels, I always make it a point to learn how to say thank you appropriately, whether it is "Danke vielmals" (Austrian), "Merci" (French), "Mulţumesc" (Romanian) or "Grazie mille" (Italian). It is important because it communicates respect.

Parents teach their small children to say thank you. They want them to learn to show appreciation at an early age because they know it is culturally important and because it will help positively shape their behaviors.

Wise employers know the value of personally thanking and praising their employees for their efforts. In a recent study, companies that excel in employee recognition are 12 times more likely to generate strong business results (*The Employee Recognition Maturity Model: A Roadmap to Strategic Recognition,* www.bersin.com/News/Content.aspx?id=16023).

Why is it so important to show and share appreciation? Beyond the obvious—that saying thank you is culturally necessary and business-savvy—there are fundamental reasons why appreciating others is important.

Sharing appreciation in your relationship:

- is smart psychology. Psychologists have demonstrated people need "positive strokes" to thrive. Without them, we become "stroke hungry" (Berne, 2011). Communicating appreciation is a great way to give your partner strokes.

- gives value to your partner. It tells her that she is important and her efforts are recognized.

- keeps the relationship healthy. Rather than taking one another for granted, saying thank you acknowledges your appreciation and your inter-dependence on one another.

- follows God's plan for relationships. God commands us to give Him thanks because it is good for us (I Thessalonians 5:18). We remember who He is and thank Him for what He does for us. In the same way, when husbands and wives appreciate one another, it helps them remember their partner's efforts and value.

Most of the people I meet are hard-working men and women who generously give of themselves to their partners and their families. They don't expect accolades or parades when they serve others, but it does feel good when they get a little recognition from their partners. Just yesterday in my office, a woman told her husband,

I don't expect a lot, but it sure feels good when you notice my efforts and share your appreciation.

The best example of a person who appreciates her partner is my wife, Barbara. This is not because I am Superman and do everything right (Ha!), nor because she wants to "butter me up" with thanks, Barbara chooses to express her appreciation of me and my efforts several times each day. She simply makes the effort to thank me for specific things I've done and also shares how she values me as a person.

Why does she share appreciation? She does so for many reasons—because she loves me and wants to encourage me, because God wants her to, because she does appreciate me, and because positive reinforcement works. Does it make me feel good? Sure, it does. Does it also motivate me to keep up the good work? You bet!

There is no magic formula how to correctly show appreciation. Most important is that your appreciation is genuine and that you verbalize it often. One married man told me in the presence of his wife, "I appreciate my wife. She should know that!"

When I turned to his wife, she replied, "but you never say so… I need WORDS!"

If you agree that you and your partner would benefit from showing more appreciation to each other, take the challenge in Exercise 2 and keep track of how often you appreciate your partner.

> ### Exercise 2 My Appreciation Box Score: How Often Do I Say Thanks?
>
> In the coming week, keep track of your progress. Each time you say "thank you" or share your appreciation to your partner in some way, give yourself 1 point.
>
> | Monday | | Friday | |
> |-----------|--|--------------|--|
> | Tuesday | | Saturday | |
> | Wednesday | | Sunday | |
> | Thursday | | Total Score: | |
>
> If you score...
> 0-6   Go back and study. You have a ways to go!
> 7-13   You are off to a good start!
> 14-21 Great progress! Keep up the good work!
> 22+   Congratulations! You are in the Appreciation Hall of Fame!

Of course, showing appreciation isn't just a matter of checking an action off your list. If it isn't genuine, your efforts will not be effective in communicating love, no matter what your box score says!

Tone: "I love you!"

Perhaps the most telling aspect of respect is how we speak with one another. Beyond the words that are said, beyond the things that are done, the tone of voice we use indicates whether we respect one another.

One of the biggest challenges Adam and Ashley had to face was the way they spoke with each other. Out of frustration, Ashley would unleash her wrath at Adam. Regardless of what was said, the manner in which she said it was harsh and demanding. Adam felt disrespected and would then either withdraw or sometimes lash back at her.

We tend to behave better and speak more respectfully in public than we do at home. When we arrive home and "let our hair down" it is easy to revert to the patterns of speaking we learned growing up. Whether the tone is demeaning, demanding, nagging, or simply unkind, it causes pain and is beneath us. We can do better than that.

The Bible confirms the importance of the tongue in describing it as a small spark that can set off a forest fire, as a rudder that directs a ship, and as a bit in a horse's mouth (James 3:3-7). How you speak to your partner can truly be a blessing or a curse.

You can show respect and love with tender words or disrespect through harsh, unkind words. A clear sign of a respectful tone of voice is whether you are kind. In this unkind world, a kind voice is unique, communicating respect and love (Ephesians 4:32).

Your challenge is to overcome your natural tendencies. As you rely on God's help, you can choose to treat the people you love the most with the respect they deserve and that you are capable of giving.

The "Set Up": How Respect leads to Success

Let's go back to the golf analogy. I live in Scottsdale, Arizona, where golf is a big deal. Many professional golfers live in the area, as well as thousands of amateur golfers. The difference between the pros and the amateurs is not in the quality of their equipment or how fancy their clothing is. The difference is in their preparation, how they "set up" before they swing.

Good golfers envision their play in their minds before they ever choose a club and step up to swing. Like many amateurs, I forget to do this. I also forget to remember the little things that will determine whether I hit the ball correctly or not.

As a couple, you can set up a healthy, successful conversation by how you begin. If you begin with respect (eye contact, smile, touch) and a friendly opening statement or question, most likely your partner will respond with respect. In contrast, if you start talking in a forceful or accusing way, your partner will likely get defensive.

As we've discovered throughout this chapter, respect is a choice. You choose how to begin a conversation, whether to purposefully respect your partner or not.

Exercise 3

In the following examples, please select whether the speaker started with respect. Then, write down how it could have been said better.

1. Issue: toilet paper

Hey! What did you do with the toilet paper?   *Respectful?* __yes __no
Better: ***Honey,*** _____?

2. Issue: money

What in the world were you thinking?   *Respectful?* __yes __no
Better: _____?

3. Issue: running late (by phone call)

Hello. I might be a few minutes late…   *Respectful?* __yes __no
Better: _____?

Summary

We've looked at three ways to verbally communicate respect, through acceptance, appreciation and tone of voice. We've also considered how the "set-up" to conversations will influence how the communication process will go.

Obviously, there are many more aspects to respecting one another that we haven't yet addressed. An important non-verbal way to respect your partner is making sure you follow through on your commitments. If you promise to do something and don't do it, it may seem disrespectful to your spouse.

Are you overwhelmed yet? Too much to remember? Too much to do in respecting one another? My advice—engage in healthy communication with God and with each other. Learn from Him and from one another how to make respect happen in your home.

Chapter 9 Project

This week, in addition to your prayer and communication times, please work on the following project:

1. From Exercise 1, summarize what I learned:

    How am I feeling respected?

    How is my partner feeling respected?

    What should improve or change?

2. From Exercise 2, how am I doing with appreciation?

    What should change?

3. Please review the sections on Tone and Set-up above.

    Summarize what I learned:

    Summarize what I could do better:

10   Radical Romance

The physical relationship is one of the most important and sensitive components in a couple's relationship. Couples long for intimate relationships in which they can express love through tenderness and passion.

Created as physical beings, we have God-given needs for companionship, touch, and sex. We

> **Real intimacy depends on truth, lovingly told, especially in the bedroom.** —*Joyce Brothers*

are wired to not only procreate, but also to physically connect with our partners and share a sense of belonging and intimacy that we share with no one else.

Challenges to Romance

As important as it is, the physical relationship can often be a source of pain and rejection. By definition, when we seek physical intimacy, we lower our defenses and become vulnerable. We expect our longings for intimacy to be met through our partners. If these expectations go unmet or if we feel used or rejected by our partners, it can be devastating.

Another challenge couples may face in their physical relationship is their past history. Many people carry baggage of bad sexual experiences in their past. Whether it involved sexual abuse as a child, rape or poor choices as a teenager or young adult, many of us have been sexually wounded.

These wounds may affect whether we feel free to enjoy a healthy sexual relationship in our marriages. If you struggle with sexual baggage or wounds, you may want to seek out a good professional counselor in your area to help you overcome your pain.

Talking openly about sex is difficult for many couples. They face the challenge of sexual inhibitions acquired in childhood. Out of response to society's rampant promiscuity, many conservative families adopt a puritan view of sex. If it is even discussed, the children gain the subtle impression that sex is bad and should be avoided. This can lead to dysfunction as the children become adults and are ill-equipped to discuss and enjoy healthy sexual relationships with their spouses.

In addition to their other challenges, Adam and Ashley struggled with their physical relationship. Or, perhaps it is better to say, their difficulties in communication and in resolving conflicts added to their sexual problems.

When Ashley was frustrated and angry with her husband, she would verbally attack him and then busy herself with household tasks. Understandably, Adam would usually withdraw when he was in trouble and do other things as well.

By avoiding one another, they became increasingly distant and disconnected, which was not the best scenario for a healthy physical relationship. At bedtime, Adam would either attempt to snuggle with Ashley and risk her rejection or he would keep his distance and become increasingly frustrated as time went on. If the avoidance continued for several days, Adam would sometimes succumb to the temptation of pornography as he sought to deal with his sexual drive. Ashley would continue to feel unloved, misunderstood, and angry.

Radically Overcome your Challenges

Regardless of whether you have baggage from your past, inhibitions from your childhood or disappointments in the past years of your marriage, these challenges can be daunting and hard to overcome.

If you follow the pattern of many couples, you'll become mired in despair. However, if you and your partner choose to do romance in a radically different way, you can learn to not only overcome your challenges but also come to thoroughly enjoy your physical relationship. Your physical relationship can become an area of strength in your relationship as you communicate and care for one another.

The physical relationship is often seen by couples as one-dimensional, having sex. However, a healthy physical relationship can be so much more: playful touches, reassuring shoulder rubs, warm hugs, sitting together, walking hand-in-hand, working on projects together, as well as passionate sex. The non-sexual touching can be as meaningful as the sexual. In fact, many couples report better sex when they first engage in plenty of non-sexual contact (Leman, 2006).

Radical romance is based on three principles: mutual acceptance, mutual service, and mutual trust. As you learn about them, seek to communicate with your partner about your needs and differences so you can develop a strong romantic relationship.

We considered acceptance in Chapter 9. Now, let's review and apply this principle to the physical relationship.

Accept one another, then, just as Christ accepted you.
—Romans 15:7

We are challenged to accept one another in the way God accepts us. How does He accept us? God doesn't accept us because we deserve to be accepted, He accepts us as we are. He accepts you with your past mistakes, your rotten thoughts, your jealousies, and your doubts and fears.

Radical Romance #1: Accept One Another.
You have the opportunity to do something radical, to accept your partner like God accepts you. Accepting one another as partners means you don't have to "fake it." You can be yourself and let your partner be herself. You choose to talk to one another and share concerns and wishes with one another.

In the context of romance, you will accept your partner with her past sexual experiences, her inhibitions, and her wounds. You will accept her, regardless of her external appearance or the hurtful words she has sometimes said. You will accept her because God accepts and loves you both and because you cherish her as your partner in life.

Exercise 1 Accept One Another Physically

What past experiences influence how you view your physical relationship with your partner?

What fears or inhibitions do you need to overcome?

For what things do you need your partner's acceptance?

The second principle is found in John 13:14-15, as Jesus spoke to His followers:

> *Now that I, your Lord and Teacher, have washed your feet, you also should wash one another's feet. I have set you an example that you should do as I have done for you.*

Here we have a practical example of how to love one another. Jesus and His disciples were headed to dinner, but there was no servant available to perform the traditional task of washing the people's feet before dinner, so Jesus did what was needed. He gave up His rights as the leader and met the needs of those He loved. It showed how He cared for them and valued them.

Radical Romance #2:   **Serve One Another**

When you choose to radically love your partner, you will choose to pay attention to her needs and help her. When showing physical affection, you will choose to learn what she likes and needs, not just what feels good to you. Serving your partner physically and caring for her wishes is an amazing way to communicate selfless, generous love.

What would that look like? For some men, that may mean offering your wife a backrub instead of demanding sex. It might mean prolonging your lovemaking so she also has time to climax. If she is exhausted, you could serve her by accepting that she is not "in the mood."

For women, serving your husband might mean offering positive words of affirmation or taking the time to cuddle, even if you have household chores on your mind. If you husband desires sex more frequently than you do, you could serve him by accommodating his wishes.

Exercise 2 How Can I Serve my Partner?

Consider how you can best serve your partner physically.

Record your ideas, then discuss them with your partner and revise them:

Radical Romance #3:   Restore your Trust in One Anther

As you learn to overcome your challenges by accepting one another and serving one another, you will pave the way to building or restoring trust in each other. Particularly in the physical relationship, where insecurities and inhibitions abound, trust in one another is vital.

People who have wounds and challenges to overcome often ask questions, such as:

- *Can I trust you?*
- *Can I count on you?*
- *Can I reveal myself to you?*
- *Is it safe to lower my defenses?*
- *Will what I say be used against me later?*
- *Will you care for me?*
- *Will this be different than my past experiences?*

How you love, accept, and serve your partner will determine to a great degree how trusting she will be and how free she will be to enjoy your physical relationship. Your goal should be for you to be the person she can trust, the person who accepts her, values her and serves her. As your relationship becomes a "safe place" where each of you can confide in one another, your romance should thrive.

The Romance Dance

It occurred to me the physical relationship is similar to dancing. Both are activities to be enjoyed together and they are both most enjoyable if you communicate together and stay on the same page. When you do the Romance Dance, remember these Top 10 things:

Top 10 Keys to the Romance Dance

1. **Communicate!**
    When you go dancing, you first decide together which dance you'll be doing, whether it is a Foxtrot, Samba, or Twist. In your physical relationship, you'll enjoy one another more if you agree whether it is time to hold hands, cuddle, or have sex. Don't assume your partner knows what you are thinking. Talk it over and stay on the same page.

2. **No "Cutting In"**
    Just like no couple likes someone else to barge in on their dance, so also your physical relationship needs to be exclusive. No couple can thrive if there are concerns about someone else in the picture. Regardless of whether it is a fling, a flirtation, an emotional affair, or pornography, don't let someone else crowd in and disrupt your sacred relationship.

    Couples with children at home need to balance time with the kids and private time for one another. Make use of your bedroom door lock so you can share intimate times without fear of interruption.

3. **Learn the Steps**
    Every dance has steps that need to be learned. Once you learn them, the dance becomes fun, fluid, and natural. In the Romance Dance, there are steps to learn as well. You and your partner have different needs and wishes. You can "learn the steps" by sharing what you like and by listening to your partner. As you understand one another, your Romance Dance will become effortless and more enjoyable.

4. **Don't Step on your Partner's Toes!**
    In dancing, you avoid stepping on your partner by paying attention to where she is and what she is currently doing. In the Romance Dance, your lovemaking will be more enjoyable as you pay attention to your partner and seek to please her. Of course, if you do "step on her toes," be quick to apologize and change your behavior.

5. **Give Feedback**
    Last year, Barbara and I learned a country dance, the Texas Two-Step. In my enthusiasm to learn, I took steps which were too long for her to keep up with. In a gentle way, she asked me to take smaller steps so we could both enjoy the dance. Later, she shared how much fun she had dancing with me.

    Whether you hug, sit on the couch together or make passionate love, let each other know what you enjoy, and if necessary, what you would like to be different. Healthy communication and positive feedback is essential to the Romance Dance.

6. **Dance Together, not Solo**
Your Romance Dance is a "two-person sport," an experience to be shared together. Similar to our discussion of partner-focused communication, instead of being self-focused, your focus needs to be not just on your meeting your own needs. As you enjoy passion together, you will bond and grow deeper in intimacy.

7. **Practice, Practice, Practice**
We have friends who are really good dancers. They took dance lessons, discussed various dances and practiced the moves together. Over time, they improved dramatically and enjoyed it immensely.

Your physical relationship doesn't need to be work, but you will probably enjoy it more when you prioritize it. When you both set a high priority on your physical connection, you will bond with one another in a special way.

8. **Frequency is your Friend**
People who enjoy dancing make the effort to dance as frequently as possible. With the physical relationship, frequency is much more important because we have physical and sexual needs. That's why God tells us to not "deprive one another" (1 Corinthians 7:5). Don't let the demands of everyday life crowd out your Romance Dance.

9. **Whisper**
When couples dance closely, they often talk quietly into one another's ears. They don't do this just because the music is loud. They whisper to enjoy an exclusive conversation. You and your partner can bond by sharing quiet, intimate conversations together. As you hug, kiss and whisper, you will enjoy intimate moments with all of the senses: touch, sight, smell, hearing, and taste.

10. **Have Fun**
Too often, couples allow the urgent demands of everyday life to take their fun away. They get so stressed and focused on accomplishing tasks that they fail to enjoy one another. While this is common to most couples, you can choose to be different.

Remember to view your partner as the special person you long for, the person who needs your touches and kisses, the person you enjoy life with. If you are "caught in a rut" as a couple, do something different to break out of the routine. Turn off the TV and the phones, play a board game together, give each other backrubs or shower together. Do whatever you need to enjoy one another.

Chapter 10 Project

This week, in addition to your prayer and communication times, please work on the following project:

1. Review this chapter, summarize what you have learned:

2. Schedule a time with your partner to read through and discuss the "10 Keys to the Romance Dance." With your partner, discuss these questions:

    Which of these keys are important in our romance dance?

    Are we stuck in a rut? What would you like to change?

    What do you want me to know?

    What I would like to share with you:

    What would make our romance more fun?

11   Radical Vision

I recently read a book by Paul Theroux, describing his overland trip through South Africa, Namibia and Angola (Theroux, 2013). The book describes his experiences and reactions to the travails of modern-day sub-Sahara Africa. After weeks on the road and being confronted with rampant poverty and hostility, he asked himself the question, "What am I doing here?"

> *The only thing worse than being blind is having sight but no vision.*
> —Helen Keller

This is an important question, not only for an author dealing with the slums of Africa, but also for every couple re-thinking their marriage. Perhaps the question for you would be better phrased,

What in the world are we doing?
What in the world are we doing with our lives?
What in the world are we doing with our marriage?

Wise money managers don't invest their funds haphazardly like a Las Vegas-style crapshoot. They do their homework and invest with purpose. They have a plan and take steps to implement their plan.

In the same way, couples need a coherent, thought-out plan—a vision for where they are headed in their relationships. Many have retirement (financial) goals and may plan out their estates (wills, trusts), but spend very little time discussing their vision.

Adam and Ashley were growing in their relationship. They had learned to communicate better with one another, they were better at conflict resolution by building consensus and they also were closer in touch with one another physically.

However, a challenge they still faced was frequently disagreeing about their priorities. Ashley's commitments to her extended family demanded much of her free time. Adam wanted weekend getaway trips with just their immediate family. Church and kids' sports commitments also competed for their time.

Adam and Ashley needed a coherent plan: how they envisioned using their time, their resources, how they wanted to raise their kids, and how they planned to develop their own relationship. They needed to develop a radical vision for their life together.

Radical Vision: Think V-V-V-V

While researching our families' genealogies, I discovered my wife had some interesting ancestors. On both sides of her family, Barbara had forefathers who crossed the Atlantic on the Mayflower. As I studied more about the Pilgrims, I learned about their vision, how it was shaped, and what compelled them to risk travelling to America.

The Pilgrims, who landed at Plymouth in 1620, came from England and Holland. They held strong **values** about their faith. They not only believed in God but felt strongly that they be allowed to worship the Lord in their simple way, free from the dominant Church of England.

This strong **value** (freedom of worship) led them to develop a **vision**, the dream of founding an independent community where they were free to worship and practice their faith without outside meddling. Ultimately, they planned a **voyage** to the New World. Leaving their old life behind, they risked everything for their **vision**. The lowly Mayflower was their **vehicle**, an unseaworthy vessel filled with 140 souls, the necessary means to an end (Philbrick, 2007).

To summarize, the Pilgrims used V-V-V-V: Values=>Vision =>Voyage =>Vehicle. Let's use this same pattern to develop and expand your vision as a couple.

Values: What is Important to You?

Each of us is confronted by choices and decisions we make daily. The decisions we make are based on the beliefs and values we hold, whether we are aware of them or not.

When you put on a scarf in the winter, it may be partly based on your beliefs and values. You may believe a scarf around your neck will prevent you from getting sick and not getting sick is something you highly value. Or, you may believe the scarf is fashionable and you value looking good out in public.

Your beliefs guide your values which influence your emotions which affect your behaviors.

Did you get that? Beliefs – values – emotions – behaviors. Many of our beliefs and values are subtle. We don't know where we got them. They are partly cultural, partly from family, partly personal, and partly worldly.

What is important to you? What do you most value in life? Would you agree that your everyday behaviors often don't match up with the things you say you value? Most of us are like that. We allow outside influences to draw us away from our core values and commitments, or we get distracted and forget what is most important.

You probably have good intentions for yourself and your family. But, even if you have great motives and good values, you are susceptible to getting those values compromised. There are dozens of forces that try to distract you or influence you each day. Let's brainstorm a bit on influences that compete with your values.

Exercise 1 What Competes with My Values

Consider the following slogans we encounter in the world. Add to the lists if you wish. Circle the values that influence you the most. Put an * by the values you want to influence you the most.

Marketing / retailers:

-"buy now, don't pay for 180 days"

-"you deserve a break today"

-"come to the happiest place on earth"

-"what happens in Vegas, stays in Vegas"

-

-

Media / film:

- beauty isn't just skin deep, it's everything.

- marriage is optional / disposable.

-"don't worry, be happy"

-

-

Society / World:

- commitment is to be avoided.

- your value is based on: a) money; b) beauty; c) power; d) a, b and c.

- bigger is better.

- embrace current politically-correct values or you are labeled "intolerant"

- home ownership

- freedom

- accumulate wealth / accumulate things

-

-

Family Values: what values did you embrace from your family?
- outward appearances are important / impress others
- hard work pays off
-
-

I hope you quickly see how easy it is for outside influences to shape your values. It is your choice whether you allow that trend to continue or whether you embark on a new path by adopting healthy, godly values. Abraham Lincoln advised,

---

Be sure you put your feet in the right place, then stand firm.

Now that you have begun thinking about your values and where they come from, let's move on to your dream.

Vision: What is Your Dream?

Last year, our Bible study group went through a DVD-series on *The Dream Giver*, by Bruce Wilkinson (Wilkinson, 2004). Over those two months of study, each one of us was challenged to re-examine our dream, what we envisioned doing in the coming years with our lives. One couple wanted to expand the reach of the non-profit ministry they directed. Another person wanted to sell his business and spend more time with his family. Another was searching for a greater purpose in life.

What is your dream? What do you hope to accomplish in the coming years with your life? Is that dream connected to the values we considered in Exercise 1?

What is your dream for your relationship? Beyond the questions of where you might live and what job you may have, what do you envision for you and your partner? What should your relationship be like? What will you do for other people?

As you have worked through Radical Relationships, I trust your vision of what you'd like your relationship to be has expanded. I hope you and your partner will work together to embrace God's plan and that you will incorporate biblical principles into your dream. For a good reminder what God wants for you, please review the Scriptures I've quoted in the previous chapters.

Your dream/vision as a couple can be as simple as seeking to grow more deeply in love by sharing and showing your love for one another daily. Or, your dream could be more extensive, such as growing your relationship, becoming effective parents, and doing something important in your world.

Whatever your vision may be, the key is to discuss it and decide it together. As you dialogue, start with the general values you both embrace, then try to get more specific about your vision for the present and the future.

Voyage: Where are We Going?

Many voyages require risk. Because of their vision, the Pilgrims risked an ocean crossing. Their goal wasn't Plymouth Rock. They risked the voyage because they needed a place to accomplish their dream.

While most visions won't require a geographical move like the Pilgrims, your voyage probably will require some risk. Your voyage may require you to change how you conduct your relationship, to be more open and patient, to forgive one another or to spend more time together. There is risk involved because there are no guarantees your efforts will be rewarded or reciprocated.

Why, then, would you want to undergo such risk? Because the payoff is fantastic and the alternative is crummy! If your partner joins you in a radically new type of relationship where you share and work toward a common vision, you will bond and have fun and thrive together. On the other hand, if you keep the status quo would either of you really be satisfied with that?

Vehicles: How do We Get There?

What is your vehicle? Choosing the right vehicle is crucial, it's where "the rubber meets the road."

What will help you and your partner reach your dream? Do you need outside counseling or a conference to improve your relationship? Perhaps a regular date night or a weekend away without the kids would be the means to help you. Or, your vehicle might be joining a Bible study group where you both are encouraged to follow the Lord and grow together.

As Adam and Ashley spent some time talking, they discovered they shared many values and were able to develop a similar vision for their relationship and family. Here is their vision statement: their values, vision, voyage and vehicles for the coming years

Adam and Ashley's: Values –> Vision –> Voyage -> Vehicles

Our Values:

- Our faith in God is central to our lives.
- We love one another and our kids.
- We seek to balance life's demands between work, kids, marriage, church, and extended family.
- We spend regular time together as a couple.
- We seek to serve others outside our family.
- We work together to use our finances wisely.

Our Vision Statement:

We seek to grow our marriage relationship so we communicate well and enjoy one another spiritually, emotionally, and physically (MARRIAGE). We want to continue parenting our children wisely, helping them become more independent and successful (FAMILY) and we plan to wisely use our resources of time and money, so we can enjoy today and be prepared for tomorrow. (RESOURCES)

Our Voyage:

1. Continue to develop our marriage by learning and by openly communicating with one another. (MARRIAGE)
2. Pay attention to each of our kids, give individual attention. (FAMILY)
3. Discuss and agree on our use of time and money. (RESOURCES)

Our Vehicles:

1. Attend a marriage seminar or read a marriage book together yearly. (MARRIAGE)
2. Weekly date nights. (MARRIAGE)
3. Pray together daily. (MARRIAGE)
4. Each parent spends monthly one-on-one time with each child. (FAMILY)
5. Weekly family game night. (FAMILY)
6. Monthly planning meeting to coordinate time, finances. (RESOURCES)

Several months ago, Barbara and I scheduled a weekend away to discuss our vision for the coming years. We followed the format of Values-Vision-Voyage-Vehicles and found it extremely helpful. My writing this book is a result of that weekend. I put off writing a book about relationships for two years because I knew it would take several months of my time. However, we determined that part of our vision is to help other couples succeed and one of the vehicles was for me to write a practical book on relationships. So, I made the time and here is the result!

I encourage you to complete the Chapter Project 11 below. It is a step-by-step process of developing your Vision Statement. If possible, please do this with your partner. I believe the time you invest on this project will serve you well for years to come.

Chapter 11 Project: Values-Vision-Voyage-Vehicles

Step 1: My Values (Parrott and Parrott, 2006)

Write several positive sentences that describe your values regarding your relationship. Include qualities of your relationship you already have or had in the past. Add qualities you wish you had.

Examples:

"Our faith is important to us."　　"We use our resources wisely."

"We love one another and our kids."　　"We enjoy spending time together."

"We have great sex."　　"We seek to serve others."

____ 1.

____ 2.

____ 3.

____ 4.

____ 5.

____ 6.

____ 7.

____ 8.

____ 9.

____ 10.

Now, review your statements and put a " √ " by the number for something that is already part of your relationship. Put a " W " for something you wish would develop in your relationship. Then, ask your partner to complete Step 1 also.

Step 2: Our Shared Values

Compare your answers from Step 1 with those of your partner. Circle the values you hold jointly, then record them here:

1.

2.

3.

4.

5.

6.

7.

8.

9.

10.

Step 3: Our Vision Statement

Discuss your dream together, then write 1-3 sentences that state your vision for your relationship for the coming years. Feel free to include plans for yourselves, your family, your careers, and your service to others.

Our Vision:

Step 4: Our Voyage

In order to reach your dream, you may need to change some things. This may involve some risk. List where you think your vision may take you, what may need to change:

-
-
-
-

Step 5: Our Vehicles

This is where you make your vision happen, where you put your plans into action. With your partner, brainstorm on the action steps you believe you'll need to take. Record your action steps here:

-
-
-

12 Radical Resources

One summer when I was a kid, I purchased a new baseball glove with my own money. It was my most prized possession. I oiled the leather and kneaded the mitt to break it in. I spent endless hours throwing baseballs up in the air and catching them with the glove. I practically slept with it.

> *We buy things we don't need with money we don't have to impress people we don't like.* —**Dave Ramsey**

Needless to say, that baseball glove was important to me. It symbolized something about me, that I was a future baseball star or, at least, was someone to be reckoned with. With that glove I believed I was someone special.

Whether you are a man or woman, a teen or a child, it's natural for things to be important to you. You value things that make life easier, like living in a warm house instead of a makeshift shelter or like owning a computer instead of a typewriter. You value things that are fun or beautiful, things that give pleasure to life. You may also value possessions which make a statement to yourself or others, like a new outfit or a sporty car.

Who Owns It?

There is nothing necessarily wrong with enjoying your resources, whether they are jewelry, houses, special abilities, vacations or bank accounts. The challenge lies in how you view and treat your time, your talents, and your treasure.

Part of the problem with resources is our confusion about who actually owns these resources. To whom do they belong? When we talk about resources we often use the words "my possessions" or "my stuff." Possessions are something we possess. They are also something we can become possessive about. This can lead to selfish thinking.

If you focus on "your" things, "your" time, and "your" abilities, you will likely have difficulty sharing these with God and with others. According to God's Word, everything belongs to God, including heaven and earth (Is 66:1-2, Ex 19:5); all animals, birds and insects (Ps. 50:10-11); and even our very selves,

---

Do you not know that your bodies are temples of the Holy Spirit, who is in you, whom you have received from God? You are not your own; you were bought at a price.
1 Corinthians. 6:19-20

Everything becomes a bit simpler when you come to recognize He is the owner and we are the stewards, or caretakers. We are to "take care of" the time, talent and treasures we have been entrusted with. Let's consider:

Radical Resources Principle #1:
It all belongs to God! You are simply a steward.

Radical Resources

Couples face a special challenge with resources because there are two people with two differing agendas about how to accumulate and use their resources. When you and your partner disagree on how to spend your money or how to use your time, it is probably because you have different priorities about what is important.

If these disagreements go unresolved, you could easily end up in a power struggle, playing "tug-of-war" over who will win, who will get to decide how much to spend on what.

However, there is another way to handle your resources, to radically share what is entrusted to you as a couple. By recognizing everything belongs to God and you are the stewards, you are well on your way toward a healthier view of resources. Now, let's continue and look at the second principle which flows from the first one:

Radical Resources Principle #2:
> **You are joint stewards—share the advantages and responsibilities together.**

Scripture teaches husbands and wives not only belong to one another (Ephesians 5:28-30), they also have authority over one another (1 Corinthians7:3-5). When you and your partner are entrusted with things, you have the opportunity and responsibility to jointly use them well.

For example, you might get a nice tax refund from the I.R.S. next year. What will you do with your windfall? Will you plan a trip to Vegas, buy a new TV or pay off the credit card balance? Will you make a decision together or will you unilaterally decide what you will do with the extra funds?

Because you may have differing agendas, it's vital that you get on the same page and stay on the same page about your resources. How you use your time, your money and your opportunities are topics every couple needs to address. You can have an on-going conversation about your resources and how best to use them.

The issue of trust quickly comes to mind, especially when it comes to money. If you don't trust him and he doesn't trust you, cooperation over resources will be difficult. Rather than reverting to the on-going struggle over who is in control, use the communication skills we've been discussing to apply Principles 1 and 2 in this chapter.

Your Self-esteem and Your Stuff

What you value is likely linked to what you believe about yourself and your possessions. There is a danger in basing your self-esteem on your resources. Let's go back to the example of Adam and Ashley.

At the root of many of their issues, Ashley was deeply insecure. She felt she never measured up to her mother's standards. She was never good enough for Mom, but she constantly tried to prove herself. She did this by believing her value as a woman was having the perfect family, a doting husband and a wonderful house filled with many nice things.

That's why she was so often demanding of Adam. She needed him to provide all of the things she felt were necessary to feel good about herself. Ashley was caught up in the rat race of building her self-esteem through things and recognition by others.

As I share Ashley's story with you, maybe you can identify with her a little. Each of us faces those feelings of insecurity and uncertainty. We feel the need to prove to ourselves and to others.

It boils down to how we measure our sense of self-esteem. Think of self-esteem as a thermometer. Just like the red liquid goes up when it gets hot and goes down when it is cold, so also our self-esteem goes up and down, based on some form of measurement.

We measure our self-esteem in a variety of ways: the subtle pressure to earn lots of money; the need to have the most talented, most well-behaved children; outward appearance; popularity in school or at work or at church; trying to impress the neighbors or the pastor or the boss or the spouse or the in-laws or yourself!

Like Ashley, many of the things we use to measure our self-esteem are external. We feel driven to perform for and to impress others. We feel compelled to collect stuff like a squirrel gathers acorns. However, we still feel inadequate and still

feel driven and still feel like we are getting nowhere in life.

If you get that sense of approval or acceptance or validation from others, you may feel good for a while. However, this will make you very dependent on others. You will literally lock into a belief system where your sense of happiness and security depends on what others think about you!

In spite of these feelings, please remember God didn't create you to be put into a system of self-doubt and insecurity. He warned us about this in 1 John 2:15-16:

Do not love the world or anything in the world. For everything in the world…comes not from the Father but from the world.

Most of us have learned from hard experience: things don't satisfy. Ashley wasn't satisfied, even though she collected many nice things. Many wealthy people in our society are empty and unhappy inside.

Possessions don't ultimately make us feel good about ourselves or improve our self-esteem or help us succeed in life. This leads us to:

Radical Resources Principle #3:
> **Don't confuse Stuff with Self-esteem.**
> **You have nothing to prove. You are already special.**

Your security as a person needs to be rooted in who you are in God's eyes. You are loved, valuable and special (Isaiah 43:1-4, 1 John 3:1, Ps.139:13-14). You don't need to prove yourself to yourself, to your partner or to anyone else.

3 Responses to Resources

Now that we've discussed the three principles, let's focus on three key traits that will help you do well with managing your resources.

1. **Be Generous**
   Since everything belongs to God and what you have has been generously entrusted to you as stewards, it's important that you are generous.

   Be generous by investing your time, treasure and talents in God's work. Be generous with one another and be generous with others who need your help. As we noted earlier, God promises to bless you richly as you generously give of your resources to others (Luke 6:38, 16:10).

2. **Be Wise**
   How you invest your time and use your money are decisions you and your partner should prayerfully consider and make together. Ask God to guide you in using your resources wisely.

3. **Dialogue**
   Because you may have differing agendas, it's vital that you get on the same page and stay on the same page about your resources.

   How you use your time, your money and your opportunities are topics every couple needs to address. Have an on-going conversation about your resources and how best to use them. Invest time to listen to one another and to reach consensus on stewarding your resources.

Exercise 1: How We View our Resources

Answer the following questions, then invite your partner to discuss them with you. Listen to one another, identifying your concerns and things to change. Seek consensus and avoid accusations.

Time:

1. Do we use our time wisely?

2. How are we generous with our time? With one another? With others?

3. What could I / we do better?

Talents:

4. Do we use our talents wisely?

5. How are we generous with our talents? With one another? With others?

6. What could I / we do better?

Treasure

7. Do we use our treasure wisely?

8. How are we generous with our treasure? With one another? With others?

9. What could I / we do better?

There are many useful aids to help you get better at managing your resources, including time management seminars and software. I've listed some good ones in the References at the end of the book (see books by Ken Blanchard and Stephen Covey) and financial planning and budgeting tools (see www.DaveRamsey.com). Regardless of the tools you use, I hope you and your partner will engage in open dialogue and will encourage one another in the wise use of the resources entrusted to you.

Chapter 12 Project

Please use the Financial Planning worksheets on the following pages to guide you and your partner in discussing and planning your monthly budget and in developing your short-term and long-term goals. (Once you've worked through this simple budget, feel free to use other financial tools available to help you budget and track your finances).

Our Monthly Budget

Income (monthly take home pay)

His: _____
Hers: _____
Other income: _____

Total Income: _____

Make Hope Come Alive!

Expenses (average monthly)

Charitable contributions/tithe: _____

Housing
Rent/mortgage: _____
H.O.A.: _____
Repairs (avg.): _____
Other expenses: _____
Total housing _____

Utilities
Telephone: _____
Electric: _____
Water: _____
Gas: _____
other: _____
Total utilities: _____

Loan/ Payments
Auto: _____
Credit cards: _____
Personal: _____
Student: _____
Other: _____
Total payments: _____

Food / Household
Household items: _____
Dining out: _____
Gas for vehicles: _____
Groceries: _____
Total Food/House: _____

Insurance
Health /Dental: _____
Auto: _____
Home: _____
Health: _____
Other: _____
Total Insurance: _____

Clothing: _____

Services
Internet: _____
Cable TV: _____
Lawn /pool/pests:_____
Other: _____
Total Services _____

Family
Childcare: _____
Child support: _____
Education /tuition:_____
Other: _____
Total Family: _____

Entertainment
Weekly date: _____
Vacation: _____
Hobbies: _____
Pets: _____
Kid's activities: _____
Total Entertainment: _____

Total Monthly Expenses _____

Monthly Surplus or Deficit _____

Short-Term Financial Goals

ex. Eliminate our credit card debt by paying $350 / month extra toward the debt.

1.

2.

3.

Long-Term Financial Goals

Remember to also plan for savings: ex. save for emergencies, auto, college, retirement, house down payment...

1.

2.

3.

4.

13   Radical Service

The Happiest People?

Who are the happiest people on Earth? According to a Gallup survey in 2012, the people of Panama are the happiest. They report having 85% positive emotions even though Panama ranks 90th among countries in Gross Domestic Product (see Gallup.com, Jon Clifton Dec 19, 2012). The same survey found Americans well down the list in the happiness quotient.

> *Those who are happiest are those who do the most for others.*
> —**Booker T. Washington**

Most of us know that once basic life needs are met, happiness is not determined by how much money you have. Happiness is also not determined by having the perfect job, the perfect house, or the perfect family.

When not pursuing material goals, many seek happiness by desiring peace (personally and in relationships) and purpose in life. Happiness, peace, and purpose are certainly important goals to have. The question remains, how do we get them? What will help move us toward having genuine happiness, lasting peace and a life of purpose and significance?

Like we have considered throughout this book, we need to adopt a radical approach to life because, if we do what comes naturally, if we conduct our lives and relationships like many other people, we won't achieve what we want to achieve.

Radical Service

The radical approach we need to achieve happiness in life is found in caring for others and generously serving them. Self-service comes naturally. Paul commented on this when he wrote in Philippians 2:21,

For everyone looks out for their own interests, not those of Jesus Christ.

When we take care of ourselves, we are self-focused. We buy what we want, do what we want and talk how we want. However, this addictive pattern of serving ourselves can make life empty and lonely.

The void which comes from self-service can be devastating as we ultimately don't achieve the purpose, peace, or happiness we so desire. In contrast, focusing on others' needs and generously serving them can produce amazing results. Though counter-intuitive, the more you give yourself to others, the happier you will be.

How does this apply to couples? Instead of focusing on and serving yourselves, you both can choose to be different than the norm, to "love one another deeply from the heart" (1 Peter 1:22).

But it can't stop there, merely caring for one another. In order to be truly others-focused, your generous service needs to flow to others as well. You and your partner can choose to build a strong relationship of mutual care and service, a platform from which you can also generously care for and serve others.

Similar to the promise we've noted in Luke 6:38, Isaiah 58:10 states,

...if you give yourself to the hungry and satisfy the desire of the afflicted, then your light will rise in darkness and your gloom will become like midday.

As you care for others and meet their needs, you will be blessed by God and will find the peace, purpose, and happiness you both desire. What motivation! Not only do others and your marriage benefit by your serving them, God promises to bless you, to improve your outlook on life and to help you experience good things in life.

Learn Your Partner

Adam and Ashley had made significant progress in their marriage. They had learned to talk about issues instead of yell about them. They had learned to cooperate with one another in their use of time and money and they had rediscovered their romance. Adam and Ashley were learning to build new levels of intimacy in their relationship.

One area that remained a challenge for them was in the area of serving one another. Although no longer so disengaged from one another, they still weren't as connected as they wished. This was due to their focus. Rather than considering one another, they often reverted back to "solo thinking," thinking about themselves instead of one another.

As we know, Ashley was often pre-occupied with projects, getting things done that were important to her. When she did think about Adam and doing something for him, she tended to do something for him that was actually something important to herself. She dusted the house "for him" and did the laundry "for him."

Although these tasks may have been important, they meant little to Adam. Ashley's performing household tasks didn't serve Adam because she had never taken the time to understand what was truly important to him. She was still serving herself and her needs for accomplishments rather than her husband.

Do you remember studying for the big exam in school? You worked hard to prepare because it was important to get a good grade. You want to succeed so you invested effort in your studies. Do you ever study your partner? If studying for a good grade was worth your time and effort, wouldn't learning about your life partner be at least as important?

What do you know about your partner? What builds him up? What energizes him?

To effectively love and serve him, you must commit to studying your partner. You will focus on his needs and dreams, his mannerisms and his habits. How is he wired? What does he like? What is important to him? The answers to these and many other questions will help you be more effective in serving him.

Exercise 1 should help you get started learning more about one another.

Exercise 1 Interview Your Partner

In order to better understand your partner, conduct a mock interview of your partner. Set up an appointment when you have 30 minutes to talk. For fun, give him a microphone (a pencil), take notes on a steno pad like a reporter… use your imagination! Use these questions to get you started:

- What is your favorite childhood memory?
- What are you most excited about in life?
- What do you most enjoy? Personally? In our relationship?
- What is most important to you in life? Why?
- What is most important to you in our relationship? Why?
- What do you long for? Personally? In our relationship?
- What is one thing you want me to understand about you?

After you have dialogued on these questions, summarize what you have learned. Share this with him, ask if you understood correctly, then record your summary here:

Now, invite your partner to ask you the same questions.

Serve Your Partner

In the best-known verse in the Bible (John 3:16) we read, "God so **loved** the world that He **gave** His only Son…" God's form of love involves action. If you love someone, you give something of value to him. You try to meet his needs. You love him by serving him.

When Adam and Ashley did Exercise 1, he discovered new things about his wife. He learned more about her wishes and her dreams, what was important to her. He also learned that she needed his regular attention or she would feel insecure and unloved.

Knowledge alone wasn't enough. Caring wasn't enough. Adam needed to love her by doing something. He started by listening to her daily, to her dreams, her fears and her frustrations. As he listened, he learned to empathize and show a new level of tenderness. Adam's simple steps of serving enabled Ashley to relax and smile more often.

How to get started serving your partner? In order to effectively serve him, you need to know about him and his needs (see **Learn your Partner** and **Exercise 1** above). Then, think about potential ways you could meet those needs.

For example, if your partner places a high value on your spending time together, serve him by doing things together. Plan a date together, go for a walk, or play a board game together. If he likes your help in getting things done (acts of service, see Chapman, 1992), volunteer to help on whatever task he is working on.

In order to be most effective, once you've come up with a list, run it by him to get his feedback and suggestions. Finally, get started serving. Even if you are uncertain whether you can meet the need or if it will be effective, just do something.

Exercise 2   Serve your Partner

What are your partner's Top 3 needs?

What can you do about them? How could you serve?

Ask your partner:
"If I did _____, would that help you?
Would that meet a need for you?"

Your Plan to Serve:

Serve Others with your Partner

Most of us have had positive and negative experiences in serving other people. I recall a mission trip to Eastern Europe that was very rewarding. There was a need my wife and I could meet, we completed the work and the people we served were very appreciative. Not only were we able to help, but it changed us as well. If only every service opportunity went that way!

I also remember trying to serve others when it didn't go so well. Sometimes my efforts were ineffective and sometimes the people I served treated me like a servant! Serving isn't always fun. We don't always get to see wonderful results…but don't give up.

Couples need to not just focus on themselves. Just as it is healthy for you to get your focus off yourself personally and serve others, service is great for couples.

Think of the good things that take place when a couple serves together: they discuss others' needs and how they can meet them, they brainstorm and develop a plan, they work together at serving and then they enjoy the moment together after they are done.

Sometimes we think of service to others as being only service projects, like volunteering for a day at Habitat for Humanity or serving at a soup kitchen or going to Mexico on a mission trip. While these projects are certainly important, serving others can also be done informally and naturally.

You and your partner can serve by watching the neighbor's kids for an afternoon, by visiting your grandmother and helping her in the home, or by inviting a family from church to your home for dinner.

I'd like to challenge you to plan to serve others with your partner. By joining together to consider others and meet their needs, you can discover a new level of bonding as a couple. Please invite your partner to do Exercise 3 with you.

Chapter 13 Project: How Can We Serve Others?

Since serving others is good for them and good for you, please consider how the two of you could serve someone.

Guidelines
Brainstorm and plan it together, serve together and then evaluate what you learned. Please remember: enjoy serving together. How you serve (together, joyfully) is as important as what you accomplish.

Brainstorm - what to do?

- What is a need we are aware of? Who needs some help?

- What could we do?

Plan - what will we do?

- We want to serve _____ by doing _____.

- When will we do it?

- What do we need to prepare?

Evaluate - How did it go?

- Did we meet a need?

- Did we enjoy serving together?

- What can we learn for next time?

Dream – Where to go from here?

- Who else needs our help?

- Other types of service to try?

14   Radical Parenting

It's been said, "parenting is the process of letting go of what you can't hold onto." As parents, we want our children to become increasingly independent. We want them to become successful young adults. Our task is to help them get there.

> *Take it easy on teenagers…they're actually good people…some of them.*
> **—A Teen to Parents.**

Effective parenting is one of the greatest challenges most adults face:

- Many parents had poor role models growing up. They learned poor communication skills and struggle with conflict resolution. They don't intuitively know how to be good parents.
- The erosion of values in society makes it difficult for parents to raise their children with healthy values.
- The rise of media in society influences youth more, leaving less room for parental influence.

Effective parenting is particularly challenging to couples because it involves two parents. Both you and your partner have your own family experiences, your own values and your own styles of relating to children. Coordinating your two approaches can be tricky and requires plenty of dialogue and cooperation.

Many couples who re-marry report that blending their two families and parenting styles together is the biggest challenge in their new marriages. The children are already accustomed to the biological parent's style. When a new parent is added to the family, differences abound: different parenting styles, different values and different family cultures. In addition, the children may have resentments toward the new parent and new sibling rivalries may develop between the step-siblings.

In spite of these challenges, failure is not an option. You want your child to be successful, you need to be effective as a parent and you desire to effectively parent together with your partner. In keeping with the theme of this book, you need a radical approach to parenting in order to reach your goal of effective parenting,

Why do we need radical parenting? Radical parenting means parenting differently than the norm. It means being different from how other couples parent their children and, perhaps, different from how your parents parented you. Radical parenting means real teamwork: you and your partner will communicate, coordinate and create as a great team in raising your child.

Communicate: Can You Hear Me Now?

Throughout this book, we've discussed communication. To thrive as couples, we need to talk on a deeper level about everything. We need to talk about our feelings, finances, and faith. We also need to discuss preferences, passion, and parenting.

As noted earlier, how you communicate with one another is a major factor on whether you will succeed as a couple. Obviously, how you communicate about your parenting roles will impact how successful you are at co-parenting your child. Here are four keys to remember about communication in parenting:

1. **Time: Take time to discuss parenting.**
   Talk about your roles, your goals and your expectations of one another. Discuss your child's current needs and what you can do to meet them. (See Exercise 1 below)

2. **Practical: Talk about the practicalities.**
   Discuss "who needs to do what now?" Keep the discussion balanced between you. Don't fall into the trap of one person solely telling the other person what to do. Remember, you are partners in parenting.

3. **Respect: Talk respectfully to one another.**
   Not only is respect essential to a healthy relationship, your child will learn more from your example than from what you tell him. If you talk to one another disrespectfully, he will likely talk to you and to his future spouse in a similar way.

4. **Talk, don't yell.**
    You need healthy communication not only with one another, but also with your children. Regardless of their ages, they need kind, respectful communication.

    In a recent interview, Dr. Nadine Kaslow, the President of APA (American Psychological Association), described how yelling at children doesn't work. Rather than getting them to hear your concerns, they will tune you out like an obnoxious commercial on TV.

    Instead of raising your voice, work hard to state your concerns and listen to the children. Not only will it help deal with the issue at hand, it will also teach them healthy ways to communicate.

Take some time to review the communication skills you worked on in Chapters 5-6. Regardless of whether you discuss vacations, money or the children, the same principles and skills apply.

Exercise 1: Let's Talk about the Kids

One important topic is that you both understand where your child is in his age-stage development. Please study this chart (Zimmerman, 1999) with your partner and answer the questions below:

Stage (yrs.)	Theme	Emotional Focus	Challenge?	What they need?	DON'T
0 - 1.5	Dependency	Bonding	So much to learn	High touch, talk, read to them	Spank
1.5 - 3	Exploration	Personal will	What is allowed?	Structure, touch, read to them	Reason
3 - 5	Communication	Social skills	Discover the real world	Let them help, read to them	Ignore, Stifle
6 – 8	Early Independence	School Society	What role to play?	Help them succeed, read to them	Overwhelm
9 - 12	"bodily functions"	Status	Fun vs. responsibility	Challenge, support	Capitulate (give in)
13–15	Peer pressure	Gender issues	Learning to think for self	Guidance, role models	Dominate
16-18	"Big-time" Independence	Separation	Where do I fit?	Freedom, listening	Withdraw

a. On the chart above, circle the stage your child currently is in. Read across the row which describes this stage. Does it "fit" with your experience? (Some children may develop faster or slower than the given age ranges.)

b. From the chart, fill in the blanks below which describe your child's stage. Then, discuss this together and add your comments. How have you observed this?

Make Hope Come Alive!

My child's name: **Stage:**

Theme:

    example:

Emotional Focus:

    example:

Challenge:

    example:

What they need:

    What we have done that works:

DON'T:

    What I can do instead:`

Coordinate: Follow the Playbook

    As I write this chapter, America is beginning another football season. Throughout the country, millions of people will focus their attention for the next five months on their team's success or lack of success in moving an oblong, leather ball down the field of play.

    Whether it involves schoolboys, NCAA teams, or well-paid professionals, the goal remains the same: to score more points than the opponents by advancing the football across the goal line. Football is a team sport, where each player has an important role in the success of his team. It requires dedication, hard work, communication and coordination.

Parenting is a lot like football, I think. No, I'm not talking about the physicality of the sport, the pushing, shoving, and tackling. Rather, parenting as a couple requires a great deal of cooperation and coordination.

Football players memorize their playbook which describes exactly what they are to do. Sometimes, a "blown play" occurs when some of the players misunderstand which play has been called. Some run one direction, others run another. Rarely do blown plays succeed. Coaches spend many hours teaching their players to coordinate with one another, so everyone is on the same page.

Most parents have experienced their own blown plays. Perhaps you can think of examples where you and your partner weren't on the same page. Just like the football players, you will benefit from working on and learning your playbook, where you are headed with your kids and what each of you will do as parents. You can stay on the same page by communicating with one another and coordinating your efforts.

Part of coordination is having the same goals, what you hope to accomplish as parents with your children. Parenting can be described as building character in your child, as stated in Proverbs 22:6:

Train a child in the way he should go, and when he is old he will not turn from it.

The biggest remaining challenge Adam and Ashley faced was in parenting. Each had his own priorities in parenting and his own way of doing things. These differences naturally led to conflict in how they would raise their kids.

Having made so much progress in other areas of their relationship, they decided to put their newly-developed communication skills to work. They discovered they had the same goals for their children, to help them succeed and grow into healthy young adults. They then focused on how to jointly make that happen.

Make Hope Come Alive!

An important part of coordination is agreeing how you will do things and understanding what role each of you plays. In essence, you need a playbook to guide you as you work together to raise your kids. Let's work on this now:

Exercise 2

Discuss your parenting together and develop your Playbook. Record your goals for your child, your roles and the things you agree are important to remember. See the example of Adam and Ashley's playbook to get you started, then write your own playbook.

Adam/Ashley's Parenting Playbook

- Our goal: to help our child succeed in life and in the things that count.
- Our roles: to help him develop in character, knowledge, skills and in his faith in God.
- We stay on the same page by constantly talking to one another.
- We back one another up.
- If we disagree about parenting, we discuss it behind closed doors.
- We talk respectfully to one another and to our child.
- When we "blow it," we huddle up and learn from it (without blaming one another).

Our Playbook

- Our goal:
- Our roles:
-
-
-
-

Create: Creative Parenting at Work

Great parenting involves creatively working together to help your child grow and thrive. Creativity in parenting sometimes takes a few extra minutes of thought and conversation, but the payoff can be tremendous for both you and your child.

In Chapter 7, Radical Resolution, you used creativity to help Adam and Ashley resolve their crisis over where to vacation. With some good listening and creative thinking, they were able to think "outside the box" and find a solution that worked for them both.

The same process of building consensus can be used in parenting. Let's see how Adam and Ashley decided to deal with Billy, their 7-year-old son, who got in a fight at school. They used the same five questions to guide their discussion (see page 65).

1. **Is this important? Do we need to agree on this?**
   Yes, we need to stay together on this.

2. **What is the issue? Identify what is the problem or the issue.**
   What to do about Billy? Should he be punished? How?

3. **Real Concern? Is there a deeper, underlying concern here?**
   Ashley: I want him to behave well.
   *   ...It shows whether I'm a good mom or not.*
   Adam: Why did he get in the fight? Did he win?
   *   ...If my kid wins, I'm a winner, too!*

4. **Creative Solutions?**
   -scold Billy about fighting.   (NO)
   -teach Billy how to fight effectively.   (NO)
   -let the school handle it.   (NO)
   -talk to Billy, ask him more about the situation.   (YES)
   -decide on his punishment after talking to him and   (YES)
   hearing his reasons.
   -teach him other ways to handle conflict.   (YES)

After some dialogue, they chose to use the last three solutions.

5. **Resolved?**
   Yes, we are on the same page about what to do with Billy.

Another way to use creativity as parents is in how you speak with your child. Most people respond better with options than with commands. Even small children like choices rather than simply being ordered to comply.

Although as parents you may want to assert your authority, with creativity you can avoid many of the power struggles and give your child small choices. For example, rather than ordering Johnny to "pick up your toys NOW because I said so!" you could give a choice: "Would you like to pick up your toys first or wash your hands first?"

With an older child, creative parenting might involve dialogue regarding his chores. After discussing the household needs and requesting his help, give him the freedom to perform the chores when he wishes. Bottom-line: think outside the box just a bit, to help everyone feel included and respected.

Chapter 14 Project

To help you review what you've learned about parenting, please complete the following and discuss it with your partner:

Communicate Together (from Exercise 1)

- Our child's development theme is:

- His/her emotional focus:

- The challenge:

- Our child's need is:

- Don't:

Cooperate: Our Playbook (Exercise 2)

- Our goal:
- Our roles:
-
-
-
-

Create: Creative Parenting

What issues in parenting are we currently facing?

How would creativity help us stay on the same page?

15   Radical Rewards

Let's be honest, we all like rewards. We teach children, if they eat their veggies, they get dessert. Workers know they will be paid on payday. Athletes train their bodies and minds, saying "no pain, no gain." They know their hard work will pay off.

> *What's in it for me?*
> *—asked by millions of people, like you and me.*

Whether young or old, we all need motivation to keep going. We need carrots dangling in front of our noses. Since it is easiest to take the path of least resistance, we need a constant reminder to tell us the momentary discomfort we face is worth it. We cling to the promise that the long-term outcome will be bright, that we'll reach our dreams and desires if we continue.

What about in your relationship? Don't you sometimes wonder, "what's in it for me?" It's a fair question: If you respect your spouse and do the dishes and go to work and talk together and take out the trash and try not to cuss and remember 50 other things, don't you ask, "what do I get out of it?" Think about your motivation by completing Exercise 1.

Exercise 1

"What's in it for you?" What has been your motivation in marriage?

How has your motivation changed in the time you have worked through this book?

There is a quick answer to "what's in it for me?" If you don't do those right things and, instead, focus only on your own needs, it is clear what you get. You will eventually have a broken relationship filled with pain and heartache.

However, let's think a bit deeper about this provocative question. Part of building a Radical Relationship is gaining a new understanding about the rewards involved. This understanding will help you develop realistic, healthy expectations of your relationship. There are three perspectives of Radical Rewards we need to consider: the spiritual perspective, the long-term perspective and the motivational perspective.

A Spiritual Perspective

Years ago, I came to the conclusion that if I do things God's way, life always turns out better. That doesn't mean I always do things God's way. I sometimes revert back to my way, i.e. the self-focused way. That way often leads me down the proverbial bunny trail, until I wake up and get back on track with God.

Early in this book, when I introduced the concept of Radical Relationships, I shared with you God's promise in Luke 6:38, "Give and it will be given to you." This theme is echoed in Isaiah 58:10-11,

> *... if you give yourself to the hungry and satisfy the desire of the afflicted, then your light will rise in darkness and the Lord will continually guide you, and satisfy your desire...you will be like a watered garden and like a spring of water whose waters do not fail.*

What's in it for you? If you give your best to God and to others, you will be blessed and cared for. God will meet your needs through your own work, through other people and through ways you can't even imagine. He is God, after all!

He also will help you to continue being a blessing to others. Part of the reward of becoming others-focused is that you will find strength and motivation to continue loving and caring for your partner. Like a top that keeps on spinning, as you help others you will be blessed and motivated to continue serving others.

Memories and Motives

Last month I attended my high school reunion. In preparation, I thumbed through our high school yearbook and was surprised by the memories which flooded back. I thought about people and events I haven't thought about for decades.

Sometimes, even the smallest memories impact us greatly. The memories of the past drive us to behave differently in the present and future. They often dictate to us what we do and why we do it. They influence our motives and what rewards we strive for.

If someone carries wounds from his past and struggles with low self-esteem, he may be strongly motivated to earn lots of money, believing he needs to prove himself to others and to himself. A woman who was rejected in her past may hesitate to bond to her husband, for fear of being rejected again. If they are not careful, their past will cause them to repeat similar behaviors over and over.

In *Boundaries for Leaders* (Cloud, 2013), clinical psychologist Henry Cloud uses the term, "learned helplessness," meaning we get so accustomed to failure that we give up even trying to change in the future. You can't simply forget your memories or your wounds, but it is important to be aware of how they influence you and your motives.

Don't be limited by your past and allow it to cause you to give up; instead, seek to rise above your past and its failures. If the memories are too painful, see help to heal them and to overcome your past. Now, let's look at another aspect of motivation.

Why do we do the things we do? Psychologists have studied, argued and formed theories about the subject of human motivations for centuries. One of the most influential was Abraham Maslow.

Maslow believed human behavior is driven by satisfying one's individual needs. In his *Hierarchy of Needs* (Maslow, 1943), he wrote we are all driven by meeting our lowest level, physical needs first, such as sleep, food and health. Then, once those needs are met, we focus on our safety needs of shelter and preventing danger.

Moving up the pyramid, once we cover the basic needs, we then address relational needs and work at building our self-esteem.

According to Maslow, the highest level of need, or motivation, is reached by the fewest. Maslow called that highest level "self-actualization," striving to achieve individual potential and maximize one's life.

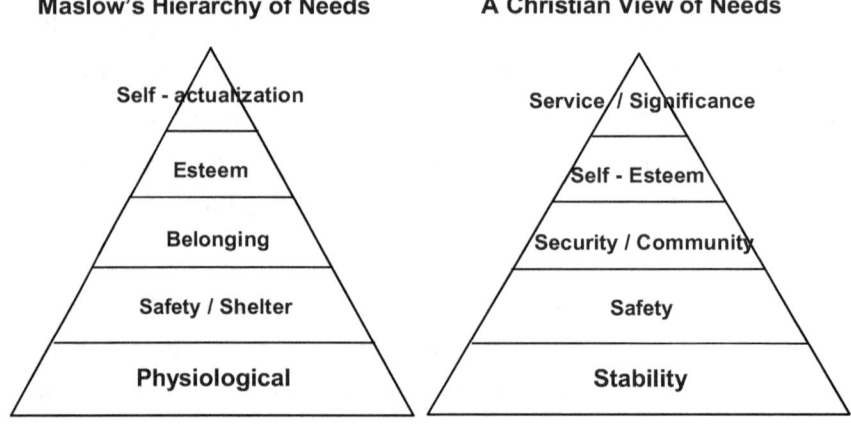

To the right, you'll see I've renamed some of Maslow's categories, based on a Christian point of view. For our purposes, you can progress in your motivation from meeting your immediate needs to establishing relationships and feeling good about yourself.

The highest motivation for the believer is not self-actualization, but service: service to God and to others, using the gifts God has given. According to both Maslow and the Bible, by generously giving of yourself to your partner, you ultimately can be happier and more fulfilled as a person and as a couple.

Long-term, Short-term

Giving of yourself to your spouse is obviously not a short-term deal. You may not get a quick reward for good behavior, like a child gets dessert for eating his peas. You may not have immediate payback if you take out the trash once or twice. However, it will pay off for you in the long-term.

I know an athlete who has been very successful in his sport of bicycling. He has biked across America, has raced up and down mountains and has trained others in cycling. He is successful as a cyclist because he is in great physical and mental shape. He is careful about what he eats, works out several times each week and rides his bike frequently as well. He has learned to discipline his mind to handle the daily rigors of training and competing. Bottom-line: his years of hard work have paid off for him.

A relationship is similar to physical training. Loving someone requires effort over an extended period of time. However, the short-term is also important. For a healthy relationship, you need to be in the moment, living for today and enjoying the moment, not just thinking about tomorrow.

What's in it for you? If you knew your efforts would pay off long-term in a healthy, loving relationship, would that be worth it? As you give your best to your partner and show that you can be counted on, your hard work and

God's blessing should have a long-term positive effect on your relationship.

Exercise 2

1. How has your work in building a Radical Relationship paid off for you?

2. How have you seen your relationship change?

3. How have you changed?

Have you followed the great progress Adam and Ashley have made in their relationship? While not perfect, I hope their story inspires and motivates you to continue to believe in and work toward your own successful relationship with your partner.

Last year, Adam was a typical guy. He had mixed motives and expectations (expected rewards). He wanted good things to happen in his marriage. He wanted his wife to be happy. He also wanted some things for himself: peace at home, no nagging from his wife and a good sex life.

Ashley also had expectations: healthy kids, growing prosperity and recognition from her friends, family and husband. She was so motivated for these rewards that she pushed herself and her husband hard to get them.

This past year, as they developed their Radical Relationship, they learned to re-examine their motives and expectations. They re-thought what drove them and they learned an amazing thing: as they selflessly cared for one another, they eventually received the rewards they personally were hoping for as well!

Adam found the best way to a good sex life was in showing his wife respect and tenderness. As he invested time talking with her and taking her seriously, she literally warmed up to him. Ashley learned a great deal about how to respect her husband. She found he was more attentive to her needs when she spoke kindly to him, rather than when she would complain, yell or nag at him.

The changes in their relationship were certainly not immediate nor did either one quickly get everything he wanted. However, the promises of God came true for them. As they gave their best to God and to one another, their relationship improved, they became a happier couple and each person experienced the long-term rewards of a Radical Relationship.

What's in it for you? What are the rewards of your Radical Relationship? Not only do you get the opportunity to develop and nourish a loving relationship with your spouse, you also get to experience the joy which comes through selflessly loving and respecting your partner. Most likely, you'll also receive kindness and love in return.

Finally, you get a new outlook on rewards, rooted in healthy spiritual, long-term and motivational perspectives. The question "what's in it for me" becomes less important. Instead you'll ask, "how can I give my best to my partner?"

Chapter 15 Project

In this final exercise, please review this chapter and write out your answers to the following questions:

1. What do I want for my relationship?

2. What do I hope for from my partner?

3. What do I want for my partner?

4. How can I give my best to my partner?

Schedule a time with your partner and share your answers. Dialogue together about how you both can improve and grow your Radical Relationship.

Final Words

Whenever I study God's Word and seek to apply it to my life, I get challenged. Sometimes, I even get a little overwhelmed—I've become aware of my deficiencies, there's still so much to learn and change. I have a ways to go!

Rather than become discouraged at my lack of progress, I try to learn from my past and thank God for the progress He has already given me in changing. I then try to focus on what I need to be doing now. Paul described this challenge when he wrote,

> *forgetting what lies behind and reaching forward to what lies ahead, I press on toward the goal.*—**Philippians 3:13-14 NASB**

From your study of *Radical Relationships*, I hope you feel motivated and better equipped to build a great relationship. I urge you to join me in learning from the past, focusing on the present opportunities to love your partner, and striving to grow a beautiful relationship in the future.

May the Lord bless you as you do your best!

References

Bersin and Associates. The Employee Recognition Maturity Model: A Roadmap to Strategic Recognition, Nov. 7, 2012., www.bersin.com/News/Content.aspx?id=16023.

Blanchard, Kenneth H., and Spencer Johnson. *The One Minute Manager*. New York: Morrow, 1982.

Carlson, Richard. *Don't Sweat the Small Stuff...and it's all small stuff*. New York: Hyperion, 1997

Chapman, Gary D. *The Five Love Languages*. Chicago: Northfield Pub., 1992.

Clifton, Jon. Dec.19, 2012. "Syrians, Iraqis Least Positive Worldwide, Latin Americans still most positive." www.Gallup.com

Cloud, Henry. *Boundaries for Leaders: Results, Relationships, and Being Ridiculously in Charge*. New York: HarperBusiness, 2013

Covey, Stephen. *7 Habits of Highly Successful People*. New York: Free Press, Rev.ed., 1989.

Kaslow, Nadine. American Psychological Association. www.nadinekaslow.com/campaign/assets/familyinterventions_2012.pdf

Leman, Kevin. *Sex Begins in the Kitchen*. Grand Rapids, MI: Revell, 2006.

Parrott, Les and Parrott, Leslie. *Saving Your Marriage Before It Starts*. Grand Rapids, MI: Zondervan, 2006.

Philbrick, Nathaniel. Mayflower: *A Story of Courage, Community, and War*. New York: Penguin Books, 2007.

Platt, David. *Radical*. Multnomah, 2010.

Ramsey, Dave. *The Total Money Makeover*. Nashville, TN: Thomas Nelson, 2003. Also, see www.DaveRamsey.com.

Steiner, Claude. *The Original Warm Fuzzy Tale*. Fawnskin, CA: Jalmar Press, 1977.

Theroux, Paul. *The Last Train to Zona Verde*. Boston: Houghton Mifflin Harcourt, 2013.

Wilkinson, Bruce. *The Dream Giver*, DVD-series. www.brucewilkinson.com, 2004.

Zimmerman, Tom. *Pro-Active Parenting*. Scottsdale, AZ: Life Changers Press, 1999.

Zimmerman, Tom. Keep the Change! Experience Lasting Life Change. Scottsdale, AZ: Life Changers Press, 2011.

Appendix 1: The Four Steps of Peace

Several years ago, I was invited to speak at a church in Sibiu, Romania. Over three days, I would address the congregation four different times. In preparation, I asked God and myself what topic would be the most meaningful.

The topic I selected was the subject of peace. I thought it would be relevant for the Romanians because their country had endured decades of hardships. Under the communist Çeaçescu regime, there was little peace to be found. Romania became a brutal police state where the basic necessities of life were unavailable, where neighbors informed on one another, and where people distrusted their government and their fellow citizens.

When I arrived at the church, I noticed there were 4 steps leading up to the platform where the pastor or other speakers would stand. On the first evening, I stood on the lowest step and talked about the 1st step in achieving peace in life. That step is seeking peace with God.

For many, this 1st step can be very difficult; however, it needn't be so hard. God wants us to have a relationship of peace and harmony with Him. He wants that so much that He did all of the hard work in establishing peace.

In spite of our unhappy, self-centered ways, God offers us peace. The Apostle Paul wrote in Ephesians 2 that Jesus Christ "is our peace" (v.14) and that He makes that peace available to us (v. 17). Jesus, the Son of God, came to establish peace between us and God by paying our debts Himself.

The only thing we need to do is to believe in Christ as the One who alone can offer peace and to accept His amazing offer of forgiveness. If you aren't at peace with God, stop right now and talk with Him. Accept His offer of forgiveness and peace. Invite Christ into your heart, then pledge to do your best in walking with Him in peace.

On the 2nd night, I moved up one step and spoke about the 2nd step of peace, that of making peace with your past. Too many of us are unable or unwilling to forgive ourselves. We get mired in our past mistakes and are unable to move ahead in life.

As I shared with the Romanians, making peace with your past comes when you realize that God accepts you, regardless of your past mistakes or failures. Romans 5:8 tells us "while we were still sinners, Christ died for us." You don't have to prove yourself to God. He loves you and accepts you as you are, so you also should accept yourself.

For my 3rd message, I climbed up to the 3rd step and spoke about the step of making peace with others, especially with those in our family. If you've worked through this book, you've already seen the value of building a loving, harmonious relationship with your partner. Naturally, this type of peace that you two are building can also be extended toward others in your life: toward your kids, your parents, your siblings and your friends.

People are often very cautious about rebuilding peace with others because it may put them in a vulnerable situation where they might get hurt again. It is certainly a risk to reach out to someone. You might get rejected or accused or misunderstood. However, it is worth the risk. Paul wrote, "If it is possible, as far as it depends on you, live at peace with everyone (Romans 12:18)."

The 4th step of peace is that of being a peacemaker, one who actively promotes peace among others. Jesus promised in Matthew 5:9, "Blessed are the peacemakers, for they will be called children of God." Being a peacemaker is synonymous with being one of God's children. If you belong to the Lord, see to it that you promote peace just like your heavenly Father does.

Join me and millions of others in seeking and promoting God's peace by taking the Four Steps of Peace today..

Walking In Wisdom

A Devotional Guide for Couples

A recent survey has shown that couples who pray and read God's Word together report a higher level of satisfaction in virtually all areas of their marriages. Another survey has shown that most Christians spend little time in prayer and even less reading the Bible each week.

Most of us want to commune with God and with our spouses, but we get distracted from nurturing these two key relationships. In our fast-paced, on-line society loving relationships have been down-sized. More than ever before, we need to reconnect to God and to each other. To do this, we need wisdom from God. We need to walk together in wisdom.

He who trusts in himself is a fool, but he who walks in wisdom is kept safe. **Proverbs 28:26**

How To Use This Guide

Walking in Wisdom is a 31-day guide to help you and your partner develop a regular Quiet Time of fellowship with God. By turning to the page which corresponds with the day of the month, you will read a passage of God's wisdom, as found in the book of Proverbs.

You and your spouse can read this together, discuss it, and then pray together. You could have your Quiet Time whenever it best fits your schedule: early in the morning, at the dinner table, or at bedtime. If your schedules don't allow, you could each read the day's reading independently and then talk about it later in the day. (Even if one of you travels often, you can still "be on the same page" with God and each other by using this guide!)

Day One

> *The fear of the LORD is the beginning of knowledge, but fools despise wisdom and discipline.* **Proverbs 1:7**

Fear is one of the realities of our society. People fear most for their job security, for their children, and for personal safety. Many of us fear an uncertain future, others fear their boss or some family member. If we are really honest, each of us probably has some phobia or fear lurking around which we wish would go away.

The fear of the Lord, though, is different. To fear God is not about being afraid of Him. It is about revering and honoring Him. Only when people recognize the greatness and wisdom of God are they prepared to really learn about life.

In contrast, foolish people are those who don't allow God to disrupt their lives. Rather than looking to Him, they choose to run their lives as though God doesn't exist.

You'll discover one of the themes in Proverbs is that we can choose whether to go the way of the foolish or to walk in wisdom. Today, you can choose which path to go down. Either you can follow the fools and their fears, or you can walk wisely by acknowledging God's rule over your life.

Consider:

If I choose to honor (fear) God today, how will that influence my perspective on today's events?

Discuss:

Have there been instances when we as a couple have been unwise by ignoring God's wisdom and direction? What did we learn from those wrong choices?

Pray:

- for a deep desire to walk together in wisdom
- for the courage to put God first in your life today.

Day Two

Thus you will walk in the ways of good men and keep to the paths of the righteous. For the upright will live in the land, and the blameless will remain in it; Proverbs 2:20-21

In the movie *Butch Cassidy and the Sundance Kid*, Butch and Sundance were backed up to a cliff while being chased by a posse. They had to make a choice: would they let the posse arrest them, or would they risk their lives by jumping 200 feet into a raging river?

Sometimes the choices we have to make seem almost as difficult. It can be very difficult to choose to live uprightly. Our society seems to reward those who choose immoral lifestyles. It can be tough to choose self-sacrifice when many others choose self-indulgence.

When you feel like Butch Cassidy and don't know which choice to make, remember these things:

1. **God's way is good**.   He wouldn't ask you to choose to obey His plan, unless it was the absolute best thing for you.
2. **God can be trusted**.   Since He promises to be with you, you can count on His help and guidance. (1 Corinthians 10:13)
3. **God will bless you**.   Short-term, it may seem that people without God do pretty well. But over the long-haul, choosing God's way is always best. (Psalm 73:2-17)

By choosing to follow Him, you can expect to "live in the land" where God rules, comforts, guides, and loves us.

Discuss:

What choices do we face this week?

Pray:

For wisdom to choose God's way.

Day Three

> *Blessed is the man who finds wisdom, for she is more profitable than silver and yields better returns than gold. She is more precious than rubies; nothing you desire can compare with her. Proverbs 3:13-15*

I have never met anyone who thinks having wisdom is a bad idea. Many people, though, have trouble seeking wisdom. It's not that we want to be unwise, we just seem to let other things influence our decisions and values. The passage tells us, our lives can be filled with priceless riches as we choose wisdom.

What would your life be like if you made it a priority to become a wise person? One of the keys to wisdom is developing habits, which help us focus our attention on God's ways. Here are some habits that will help:

- **Listen to God every day**.
  This devotional guide can help you get started.

- **Surround yourself with wise people** who share your values.

- **Don't compromise**. If you know what is right, do it.

Discuss:

Is wisdom a priority for us? What habits do we need to develop?

Pray:

Ask God to help you both become wise.

Day Four

Above all else, guard your heart, for it is the wellspring of life.
Proverbs 4:23

Most of us realize that accumulating possessions and status aren't really the signs of a happy, fulfilled life. What many of us don't recognize is the need to promote life by protecting our most valuable possession: the heart.

Just as your physical heart is the most vital organ to your body, your spiritual heart is the key to developing spiritual and relational health. As the proverb states, your heart is the source for lasting joy in life. If you care for it, you will experience these joys. If you neglect your heart, your opportunities for joy and satisfaction in life will vanish. Just like turning off the water faucet, a heart uncared for dries up and shrivels.

Guard your heart:	**How**
• Temptations:	God's Word: use it as your guide.
• Hardness of heart.	God's Love: focus on it.
• Helplessness:	God's Son: Remember Jesus. He offers us forgiveness, life, hope.

Discuss:

What should we guard our hearts against? How do we do that?

Pray:

-for an awareness of what to protect your heart against.

Day Five

*For a man's ways are in full view of the LORD,
and He examines all his paths.   Proverbs 5:21*

Do you ever think about the fact that God is watching you right now? It gives me a funny feeling when I realize how much He knows about me. Even though I may fool others, God knows what I am really like, what I think about, when no one else is around.

If God were physically by your side today, how would it change how you conduct yourself? Would you talk differently with others? Would you use your time in the same way? This proverb reminds us that He is really there right now: watching you, guiding you, sharing life with you.

Discuss:

Since He is with us right now, what difference should that make in our relationship?

Pray:

to keep the perspective that He is always there with you.

Day Six

How long will you lie there, you sluggard? When will you get up from your sleep? A little sleep, a little slumber, a little folding of the hands to rest and poverty will come on you like a bandit and scarcity like an armed man.   *Proverbs 6:9-11*

Many of us are faced with two temptations: laziness or workaholism! There have been times when I have given too much of my time and self to my job. In those times, my wife and kids suffered. They didn't receive the tender attention they needed. My out-of-balance work habits hurt my family relationships.

This proverb warns that the opposite tendency can be just as detrimental to yourself and your relationships. If you are discouraged, it can be tempting to avoid your problems and stay in bed. Or, you might be tempted to give up trying, to take it easy and indulge yourself. While we all need adequate emotional and physical rest, an over-indulgence in sleep and rest usually won't help you feel better.

In those times, you may need a renewed perspective on life and hope for the future. When you get discouraged, remember there are 3 people to turn to.

God: keep a list of favorite Bible passages that uplift you. Try some of mine: Ps.1, Ps.73, Is.40-43

Partner: Ask your spouse to listen, but don't put him/her under pressure to solve all your problems.

Friends: It is important to have 1-3 people who will listen to you without judging you.

Pray:

For a good attitude about work and a healthy balance in life.

Day Seven

> *My son, keep my words and store up my commands within you. Proverbs 7:1*

Have you ever watched a squirrel gather and store up nuts for the winter? It busily hunts, drags, and hides its supply. Sometimes they even forget where they have hidden all of their precious treasures. The squirrels have a built-in instinct to prepare for the future.

When I was a new Christian, I was taught the importance of "hiding God's Word in my heart" by memorizing Bible verses. In those first years I memorized hundreds of verses and devoted countless hours studying those little memory cards so I wouldn't forget them. In the midst of this good activity I missed the point. I focussed so much on memorizing, I forgot the reason why God wants us to keep His Word close to us.

Just like the squirrels, we need to be prepared for the future. You may not have cold winters where you live, but you will face times of trial and temptation. God calls us to prepare for them by "storing up" His Word. As you seek the wisdom found in the Bible, you'll be prepared for those challenging times ahead.

Discuss:

Is there an area of your life where you face a coming challenge?
What wisdom from God applies to that challenge?

Pray:

Ask God to help you make wise choices in the coming weeks.

Day Eight

Choose my instruction instead of silver, knowledge rather than choice gold, for wisdom is more precious than rubies, and nothing you desire can compare with her.   Proverbs 8:10-11

We often long for things that are really unimportant. In hindsight, it may even seem silly that these things, activities or accomplishments were so important to us. I laugh at my wishlist from 20 years ago.

While some of the things we strive for are fine dreams, many of them are not things God has told us to pursue. In contrast, there is one thing each of us urgently needs: wisdom.

Discuss:

Do I/we want to become wise?
What are we willing to risk?
How would our life be different if we became wiser?
What difference would it make in our family?

Pray:

Ask Him to help you desire wisdom more than possessions.

Day Nine

Instruct a wise man and he will be wiser still; teach a righteous man and he will add to his learning. Proverbs 9:9

I once read several different biographies of Abraham Lincoln and was amazed at how often he failed in life. He was unsuccessful as a farm hand. He failed twice as a shop owner. His law practice didn't make much money in the first years. He also lost most of the elections he ran in, including a bid for the Senate in 1858.

As I read about his failures, I was even more impressed at how he learned from situations and people. Lincoln continued to grow as a person. This helped him as he led his nation through five years of war and civil unrest.

As the proverb reminds us, a wise person actively seeks to learn and grow in wisdom. Jesus described his followers as learners, or disciples, and challenged them to grow. I have a friend who repeatedly makes the same mistakes because he didn't learn from past mistakes. He doesn't listen to wise friends when they warn him. The Bible calls this type of person a fool.

You choose whether you want to develop wisdom. If you want to grow in wisdom, you will learn from God's Word, from God's people, and from the life situations you encounter.

Discuss:

Are we developing a lifestyle of learning?
Do we become wiser through the people and situations God brings into our lives?

Pray:

- that you will learn from your mistakes, as a disciple of Jesus.

Day Ten

The man of integrity walks securely, but he who takes crooked paths will be found out.   *Proverbs 10:9*

Integrity: a four-syllable word describing a concept that sounds good, but is impossible to practice in today's world.

Do you agree with this definition? Most people agree that telling the truth is generally important, but many believe there is a limit to how truthful one must be. "Honesty is good, when it fits the occasion!"

A better definition of integrity is speaking and living out truth. It involves dealing with others in an honest, above-board way. This may sound old-fashioned and out of step with our fast-paced society, but it is God's way. He is all about truth, the truth of the gospel and of Scripture. His own nature is truth.

Integrity is not just a command. It is good for us and is a key building block for healthy relationships. If you choose to be honest with others, your relationships will thrive and God will bless you. If you are known for integrity, others will trust you and be drawn to you.

Discuss:

Who do we know who frequently lies?
What are his/her relationships like?
Is our relationship built on integrity?

Pray:

For a growing relationship between you and your spouse, in which you can be open and honest with each other.

Day Eleven

A generous man will prosper; he who refreshes others will himself be refreshed. **Proverbs 11:25**

Since moving to the desert of Arizona, I have begun to appreciate water in a new way. Perhaps I notice water more now because of the harsh, dry environment. I know I need water to survive. I watch with fascination as each plant and animal in the desert seeks out a way to secure an adequate source of moisture.

People also are visibly drawn to seek out water for cooling refreshment. I have a friend I always look forward to seeing. I know he sincerely cares about me. He listens carefully and seeks to encourage and help whomever he can. Just like water in the desert, he refreshes others.

Notice God's promise: if you choose to refresh others, God will care for and refresh you. The more generous you are in giving love to others, the more God will sustain you. "Give and it will be given to you (Luke 6:38)." That is His way of blessing.

Couples have a special opportunity to refresh one another. You can be a refreshing source of God's grace for your partner, as you choose to build into your mate.

Consider:

What special need in my partner's life could I meet today?
Who are people we, as a couple, could refresh? What could we do?

Pray:

Ask God to help you see opportunities to refresh others today.

Day Twelve

A wife of noble character is her husband's crown.
Proverbs 12:4

We live in an area where many people invest large amounts of their time and money in purchasing and maintaining a large house. That is what they value. When I lived in Germany, I was impressed with the amount of time men would spend cleaning their Mercedes-Benz. They valued having a spotless luxury car.

In the past years, Barbara and I have faced several crisis situations where we were at the end of our rope. In those times, I learned the value of having a wife of noble character, one who is focused on walking with God and on reflecting His character in her life. In each situation, I became very thankful for having a partner I could rely on.

Consider:

What do you value most? Possessions? Career? Reputation?
What about becoming a person of strong character? How important is that?

Discuss:

Spend a few moments sharing how you appreciate your partner. Then, discuss ways each of you might continue to grow in godliness.

Pray:

For God to help you value and grow in godliness.

Day Thirteen

Hope deferred makes the heart sick, but a longing fulfilled is a tree of life.   Proverbs 13:12

I recently counseled a couple who wants to improve their marriage. They have good intentions, but they don't follow through with the right actions. Too often, the husband has disappointed his wife by not following through on his promises. Out of her hurt, the wife responds by withholding her love from her husband. Because of procrastination they are caught in a vicious cycle.

From this proverb, we learn that procrastination is more than a mild character flaw. When we put off our dreams, something dies inside us. We get caught up in disappointment and despair. Instead of hope, we get depressed.

In contrast, think about those times when you followed through well and finished what you had intended. Do you remember that sense of joy? It is a "tree of life" to complete what God directs you to do.

You have the great opportunity to help you and your partner develop deep joy. Good follow-through sends good messages. As you actively seek to meet your spouse's needs, you demonstrate your love. By following through on your promises, you show how much you care.

Consider:
Is there something I have been putting off that I should care for today?

Discuss:
What can I do to encourage you this week?

Pray:
Ask God to help you change procrastination into follow-through.

Day Fourteen

A heart at peace gives life to the body, but envy rots the bones.
Proverbs 14:30

After two major wars in the past decade, we long for peace. Yet, our society doesn't seem to be very peaceful. Drive-by shootings occur hourly, cases of domestic violence are at an all-time high. We really live in the age of rage, where anger rules many relationships.

Jesus taught much about peace, but was frequently misunderstood. His teaching, "blessed are the peacemakers," requires that we personally experience peace if we are to promote peace with others. Each of us needs peace on 3 levels: peace with God, peace with the key people in your life, and peace with your world.

You can begin to experience peace by finding peace with God. If you turn to Jesus in faith and give Him control of your life, you can begin a lasting relationship with God. He cares deeply for you and wants you to feel loved and at peace. Get started by praying and talking to Him about these things.

A Sample Prayer:

"Father, in the past I haven't lived at peace with you. I have tried to do things my way, even though Your way is better. I have made wrong choices and hurt other people. I believe in Your Son Jesus, who is able to pay for my sin. Would You please forgive me? From here on, I want to live my life in peaceful fellowship with You. Please help me do this. Thank you. Amen."

(For more information on developing peace in your life, see Appendix 1.)

Day Fifteen

> *The tongue that brings healing is a tree of life, but a deceitful tongue crushes the spirit.* **Proverbs 15:4**

Last week, I met with two influential men. The first man is known as a great public communicator. I noticed his comments seem to have a harsh, critical edge to them. I came away from the conversation feeling drained. The next day I met with the second man. Although he is less widely known, I was personally impressed. His speech conveyed a positive, caring attitude toward people. I enjoyed being in his presence and look forward to future meetings.

Have you ever noticed how the tongue, such a small part of the body, can influence your life in such a major way? Your speech greatly influences how successful you will be in relationships with others.

According to the proverb, people who communicate acceptance and healing are great to be around. They add to others' lives by bringing encouragement and joy. Your relationship with your partner can be greatly enhanced if you learn to apply this verse. The following 3 "H's" may help:

- **HONEST** Determine to always be truthful to your partner.

- **HEAL** Look for opportunities to build up your partner by focusing on his/her positive traits.

- **HEART** We speak from our hearts. As you focus on God, allowing Him to influence your heart, you can better love and encourage your spouse.

Consider:
What healing words can I share with him/her today?

Pray:
For the strength to speak words of healing to your loved ones.

Day Sixteen

> *Commit to the Lord whatever you do, and your plans will succeed. Proverbs 16:3*

I don't know anyone who doesn't want to be successful. It's natural that we want everything in life to go as planned and to have great results. That is why this passage is great news—that our plans will succeed!

There is a common theme throughout Proverbs, and the Bible as a whole: People are near-sighted! We quickly plan out our lives and decide what would be best for us (short-sighted), without considering that our Creator might have different, better plans for us (the big picture).

What does this verse mean for us?

When you commit something to God, you do it for His honor. If it doesn't honor Him, better not do it. You need God's perspective on your life and your daily decisions. You need to reorient yourself by listening to Him each day.

If you daily yield your plans, hopes, and dreams to Him, He will speak. If your ideas fit His plan, great. If He has something better, you need to know that. This doesn't just apply to life's big decisions. God is interested in all aspects of your lives.

Discuss:
What have we seen God bless, as we commit it to Him?

What other areas of our lives do we need to commit to Him?

Pray:
Ask Him to give you both insight in committing your lives to Him.

Day Seventeen

He who covers over an offense promotes love, but whoever repeats the matter separates close friends. Proverbs 17:9

Have you ever made a mistake which has hurt someone else, who in turn tries to hurt you back? Most of us have seen that sad, ugly cycle repeat over and over. Revenge or repeat hurting ruins the strongest relationships. Perhaps you have hurt someone, only to have them turn and forgive you? How did that feel? Besides feeling ashamed, you probably felt closer to that person and grateful for the forgiveness.

You and your partner will inevitably hurt each other, but forgiveness allows you the opportunity to turn something sad into something very beautiful. Forgiveness is probably the single most powerful thing God has given couples to build strong marriages.

Forgiveness is releasing someone from the wrong they have caused. As the proverb states, it is "covering over" an offense. This is much different than a "cover-up" in which we try to hide our sin. To cover over, or forgive, a sin means that both parties agree that it was wrong. Then, the offender needs to express true remorse about it. Finally, the offended person forgives the offender, allowing love to take the place of the pain.

Discuss:
Ask your partner: "Is there something I have done to hurt you?"
Make sure you understand your partner's feelings, then express remorse and ask forgiveness.

Pray:
For a sensitive, forgiving heart.

Day Eighteen

Before his downfall a man's heart is proud, but humility comes before honor.   *Proverbs 18:12*

Pride: thinking highly of myself and my abilities; the tendency to elevate my own importance.

Humility: keeping the proper perspective of who God is and who I am.

Personal pride can be a very positive trait. It can help you succeed in your career. Most employers want their employees to have high standards and the desire to achieve. There is another type of pride that can keep us from success in life. Destructive pride comes when we lose the proper perspective about who we are. We have the natural tendency to inflate our own importance. When we are "proud of heart," we easily forget about God and other people.

In contrast, a humble person is someone who remembers that God is all-powerful and all-loving. This person views himself as an important part of God's overall plan. Throughout Scripture, God has promised to support those who remain humble, "Those who honor me I will honor." -1 Sam.2:30.

Discuss:

Who do we know who has a good balance between personal pride and humility?

What can we learn from his/her example?

Pray:

For the wisdom to keep God in the middle of your lives.

Day Nineteen

What a man desires is unfailing love; better to be poor than a liar.   Proverbs 19:22

What is it you really want? What is on your "wish list?" Take a moment and jot down some of the things you'd like to own or experience, but don't yet have:

Now look at your list again. How many of those items are things that reflect a deeper need you may have? Circle those. Would you agree with the proverb, that we all have a deep need to be loved and accepted? Faithful, unconditional love – what could be more important?

Relationships usually thrive or fail, depending on whether the couple shares generous, unconditional love with one another. You have the opportunity to choose each day what is most important to you, whether it is things, accomplishments, activities or expressing love to your partner.

Consider:

How do I express unconditional love for my partner?
What needs does he/she have that I can meet?

Discuss:

What needs do you have that I can help meet?

Pray:

Thank God for His unfailing love.

Day Twenty

Many a man claims to have unfailing love, but a faithful man who can find?   Proverbs 20:6

Our family once visited the world-famous San Diego Zoo. Of all the exotic animals, the biggest crowd-pleasers are usually the smallest, the baby animals. People lined up to gawk at the baby monkeys, gazelles, giraffes, and a sleeping baby lynx.

What impressed me most were the baby animals' parents. Wherever there was a little helpless creature, nearby there also was a protective adult carefully watching over its offspring and attending to its needs. Each of these animals exhibited faithfulness, a lifestyle of dependability and service.

One of our most urgent needs today is for faithfulness. We need teachers and public officials we can count on. Kids need parents who will faithfully love and care for them. To be successfully married, husbands and wives need to know they can depend on their partners.

By following these three steps, you can follow the path of faithfulness and become one of those faithful men and women that are so hard to find.

1. **Confess** to God and your partner that it is beyond your power to be faithful. You need God's help. Ps. 127:1, Zechariah 4:6

2. **Consider** what steps you can take today. What does it mean to live out faithfulness before your partner? At work? In the neighborhood?

3. **Choose** to be faithful today by changing one action / behavior which is consistent with God's call to faithfulness. Then, build on this by working on another area tomorrow and another the following day.

Day Twenty - One

He who pursues righteousness and love finds life, prosperity and honor.   Proverbs 21:21

We all know that the Bible is filled with instructions about how to live righteously. The Book of Proverbs, in particular, focuses on this theme. Have you ever considered the connection between righteousness and love? According to verse 21, right living and right loving are things that go together. Can you imagine the results of doing one without the other?

On a long trip, a woman might focus on observing every traffic law, never speeding, but at the same time verbally abuse her husband and children in the car with her. A man might profess great love for his family, yet commit moral indiscretions which tear at the very fabric of the family he loves.

We can't really live righteously without loving those around us. And, we can't successfully love others if we aren't committed to living rightly before God. Just as we should pursue doing what is right, we also need to develop a lifestyle of loving others.

The payoff for living right and loving right is so great. Let's pursue righteousness and love today!

Discuss:

What is something we need to change in our pursuit of righteousness?

Pray:

For your marriage to be built on right living and right loving.

Day Twenty - Two

A generous man will himself essed, for he shares his food with the poor.   Proverbs *be bl 22:9*

Generosity is one of the key ingredients toward building healthy relationships. In my counseling ministry, I have seen that happy couples have learned the value of generously sharing with one another. They give their time, possessions, love, and forgiveness without keeping track of what they will receive in return.

Sharing also helps us to keep the right perspective on life. When we give to others, we acknowledge that all that we have ultimately comes from God. He entrusts things to us to use wisely and to share. Generosity doesn't come naturally, does it? You have to work at it. Here are three ways to become a generous person:

RECEIVE gifts graciously. Give thanks to God and people as often as you can. It will help you remember that you have received much.

RESPOND to God's gifts by sharing them with others. A goal for you may be to give 10% of your income and 4 hours/week of your time to His work.

RENEW your relationships by "giving back more than you take out." In the same way you should deposit more in your bank account than you withdraw, so also you can add to your "relationship account" through generous giving.

Discuss:
Express your appreciation for your partner's generosity. Ask him/her for tips in becoming better at generous giving.

Pray:
Thank God for His generous gifts. Ask Him to help you become more generous.

Day Twenty - Three

*There is surely a future hope for you,
and your hope will not be cut off.* **Proverbs 23:18**

Have you ever hoped that things will get better? It is part of our nature to want a future filled with good things. Each generation promises us a rosy future. Think about some of the messages of hope we heard in popular songs of the past years:

"it's gonna be a bright, bright sunshiny day" (70's)
"there's gonna be a morning after" (80's)
"don't worry, be happy" (90's)

Most people know it takes more than a cute song to build a bright tomorrow. Wisdom tells us that trusting in chance or in our own abilities also can't guarantee us future hope.

God's promises are different. They aren't happy little words without substance, but are based on His own nature. Throughout the scriptures, He promises a future of hope to those who choose to pattern their lives after His design. Consider the following ABC's for hope today:

A - **Acknowledge** that your future depends on God. He offers you forgiveness, salvation, and lasting peace as you commit your life to Him.

B - **Believe** that God will keep His Word. If you trust Him and pattern your life after Him, He promises you a great future. (Jeremiah 29:11)

C - **Choose** to act on hope. Even if you don't yet feel very encouraged, get busy doing the right things now. The feelings of joy and hope are just around the corner. As you live right and love others, God will help you regain hope.

Day Twenty - Four

If you falter in times of trouble, how small is your strength?
Proverbs 24:10

When our daughter was very young, I gently warned her to not to get into trouble by disobeying. She responded, "Where is trouble, Daddy?" She wasn't sure what trouble was, but she knew she better find out where it was so she could avoid it! We want to avoid trouble; yet, we know that difficulties are built into life. You can't really avoid all of them.

Barbara and I went through the crisis of our lives when our youngest child died. There was no specific way to prepare for that, except that we had already developed a deep faith in God and a close bond to each other. These strengths helped us wade through the deep waters.

Since we know trouble will sometimes come our way, our focus should be on developing strength to withstand the hard times ahead. The Bible is filled with everyday people who fought adversity (see Hebrews 11). Through strong faith and strong relationships, they were able to overcome.

You can grow strong by developing a rock-solid faith. Begin by communing with God each day. Add to your strength by applying His Word to your closest relationships. Treat your loved ones like God treats you. As you build up your strength, God will prepare you for the uncertainties ahead. Your strength will also lead you to a richer, more fulfilling life right now.

Discuss:
How can we help each other grow in strength?

Pray:
"Father, would You please help us grow strong in our faith in You and in our love for each other?"

Day Twenty - Five

A word aptly spoken is like apples of gold in settings of silver.
Proverbs 25:11

Talking to God about the Words we say...

"You are right, again. I know I got a little out of line – no, way out of line. I shouldn't have spoken to her in that way– No, she didn't have it coming, but I sure let her have it. I just wish I could take back some of the things I said."

"Sometimes it seems like we escalate the pain. I react to him, then he reacts to what I say– Why is it that the person I love the most is the same person whom I hurt the most?"

"Too often I just don't think about what my words will do to her. I just blurt out my latest thoughts without taking her into account. I know I should stop and ask myself: Is this a good time to bring this up? Am I ready to share this in a loving way? Have I prayed about this yet?"

"I agree with you that words are very powerful. Would you please help me learn to use words wisely to build my partner up? I want to be a blessing to others in what I say."

Discuss:

Speak about a specific instance when you have hurt one another with your words: acknowledge it was wrong and ask forgiveness.
What needs do you have that I can help meet?

Pray:

Have you said hurtful things to others recently? Admit them to Him, ask His forgiveness and His help in changing your words.

Day Twenty - Six

A malicious man disguises himself with his lips, but in his heart he harbors deceit, though his speech is charming, do not believe him. Proverbs 26:24-25

Yesterday we focused on how we use words. Today's text points out the connection between what is in your heart and what you say.

Do you know someone who is "malicious," who tears people down with his words? According to these verses, what people say is a reflection of what is going on in their hearts. If a person verbally assaults others, he probably is filled with negative, painful things deep inside.

How do you keep from becoming such a person? Take care of your heart. If you allow negative thoughts and emotions to roam free in your heart, you will hurt others with your words. If your heart is filled with good things, you will be a blessing to those around you.

How to heal a hurting heart:

Pray   Ask God each day to heal your heart and take away the pain.

Sing   Music is a wonderful healer. Try this chorus:
*Change my heart, O God. Make it ever true.
Change my heart, O God. May it be like you.*

Share Find someone who will take you seriously and listen to your hurts. Ask them to pray with you and help you heal.

Discuss:
How are we doing at filling our hearts with good things? How do our television viewing habits help or hinder our care for our hearts?

Pray:
Ask God to help each of you develop healthy hearts.

Day Twenty - Seven

As iron sharpens iron, so one man sharpens another.
Proverbs 27:17

Have you ever reached into the knife drawer, only to find a bunch of dull ones? Over time, knives naturally loose their edge. To be most effective, they need periodic sharpening.

We need to stay sharp too…as Christians, as parents, as partners. As the proverb teaches, God uses other people in our lives. They often are the whetstone in the process of honing and sharpening. The wise person will surround himself with people like this, so God can do His work.

Many people have recently rediscovered the important role others play in sharpening their lives. Millions of men and women meet in groups each week to grow and be accountable: Bible studies, support groups, accountability groups.

Discuss:

Who are the people we trust who can help sharpen us?
Whom are we helping sharpen?

Pray:

Ask God to sharpen you to become even more useful in His Kingdom.

Day Twenty - Eight

He who conceals his sins does not prosper, but whoever confesses and renounces them finds mercy. **Proverbs 28:13**

I have a confession to make. I don't really like the idea of confession. I don't mean the type where you go into a little closet and tell a priest about your wrong deeds. I'm talking about confessing to God what I have done that has hurt Him or other people. It is usually fairly easy to talk in generalities about my faults. "Lord, forgive me for anything I might have done to anyone." However, it is much harder to admit to God or to the ones I have hurt how wrong I was.

Even though confession is a subject we like to avoid, God tells us it is crucial that we don't. There are at least three reasons why confessing your sin will be good for you. Confessing your sin will help you:

- **receive** forgiveness   (1 John 1:9)
- **rebuild** broken relationships   (James 5:16)
- **renew** your perspective   (Nehemiah 1:6)

While it is tempting to make excuses for your mistakes, it is much better for you and others to humbly admit them and then to seek forgiveness. God promises His mercy and blessings to everyone who takes this step.

Discuss:
How have we seen our relationship grow as we confess to each other and forgive one another?

Pray:
Ask God to reveal to you what you need to confess to Him and what you need to confess to your partner.

Day Twenty - Nine

A fool gives full vent to his anger, but a wise man keeps himself under *control. An angry man stirs up dissension and a hot-tempered one commits many sins.*   *Proverbs 29:11, 22*

When was the last time you got really angry? If you are like me, you'd rather forget about that episode. Even though we regret it, why do we give way to those anger outbursts? Consider some of these facts about anger:

- unchecked anger is an emotion out of control.
- anger can be directed inward against yourself (leads to depression)
  or outward toward others (leads to hurt relationships, rage).
- unchecked anger has the potential to damage or destroy relationships very quickly.
- anger is a secondary emotion, fueled by the primary emotions of hurt and pain.
- prolonged anger is bad for your physical health.
- anger is a choice you make (no one can force you to anger).

From emotional pain, we often lash out at those we love. In those times, we need love and comfort from God and others, instead of getting caught up in anger. The next time you feel anger about to take over your life, remember the anger traffic light:

Red   - Stop and think: why am I angry?
Yellow - Consider: what options do I have?
Green   - Go: choose a positive way of expressing your emotions

Pray:
Ask Him to help you learn to deal with your anger.

Day Thirty

> *Every word of God is flawless; He is a shield to those who take refuge in Him.*   *Proverbs 30:5*

Both of these statements are fundamental to Christianity, but what do they have to do with each other? Why are these thoughts in the same proverb?

The first part talks about God's Word. It is true and without error. What He says is right. We can count on it. The second part deals with His ability to care for us. God protects those who run to Him. Like a warrior depends on his shield in battle, we can totally rely on Him.

But what if God promised something He couldn't deliver? What if He pledged to protect you, but didn't follow through? Then, neither His Word nor His promises for protection would be reliable.

Many Christians intellectually believe God and His promises, but are afraid to test them out in real life. Maybe they are afraid God didn't really intend for us to literally take Him at His Word. Instead, they give lip service to their faith, but work out their problems on their own.

In the past 20 years, I have talked with thousands of people about the challenges they face in life. The people who really count on God to help them are happier and deal with their problems better than those who rely solely on their own resources.

You and your partner have the opportunity to look to your Creator as the One who knows you best and loves you most. Trust Him to help today.

Discuss:
What is the #1 area in our lives where we need God's help?

Pray:
Ask God to help you grow in relying on Him when you face challenges.

Day Thirty - One

A wife of noble character... Her husband has full confidence in her and lacks nothing... She brings him good, not harm, all the days of her life. She is clothed with strength and dignity; she can laugh at the days to come.   Proverbs 31:10, 11, 25

I have always been fascinated with the 31st chapter of Proverbs because it describes my wife. Barbara isn't perfect, but she is godly. Many years ago she chose to allow God to change her. She wanted to become more like Him: more loving, caring, and righteous. Her faithfulness in following Him has paid off, especially for me. She is a blessing to be around.

Men: As you read this passage, does some of it describe your wife? If so, you are experiencing God's blessing. Thank God each day for her. Don't take her for granted. Let her know how much you appreciate her. Complement her in front of others. Look for ways to encourage her. Lighten her load. As you love her, you also are loving God.

Women: You may feel you don't measure up to the ideals of Proverbs 31. That's ok. You and your partner are in a growth process. The key to godly character is a deep inner walk with Him. He is there for you. Talk with Him throughout the day. Draw strength from Him. Ask Him to give you love and patience for others.

Discuss:
Share your appreciation and affection for your partner today.

Pray:
Ask God to help you both become more like the Proverbs 31 couple.

Make Hope Come Alive!

What's Next for Devotions?   Try These Passages!

Congratulations! You have completed one month of Quiet Times with your partner. I hope this experience has helped you connect with your spouse on a deeper level. Please continue to read God's Word and discuss it together. To help you, try the suggested passages below for the next three months. Then, use the Walking in Wisdom guide again for Month 4.

Day	Month 1	Month 2	Month 3
1	Ps.1:1-3	Mark 1:1-20	Philippians 1:1-11
2	Ps.8	Mark 1:21-45	Philippians 1:12-26
3	Ps.18:1-3	Mark 2:1-17	Philippians 1:27-30
4	Ps.25:1-7	Mark 2:18-28	Philippians 2:1-4
5	Ps.25:8-22	Mark 3:1-19	Philippians 2:5-11
6	Ps.27:1-6	Mark 3:20-35	Philippians 2:12-18
7	Ps.37:1-7	Mark 4:1-20	Philippians 2:19-30
8	Ps.40:1-4	Mark 4:21-41	Philippians 3:1-11
9	Ps. 42:1-2	Mark 5:1-20	Philippians 3:12-21
10	Ps.46	Mark 5:21-43	Philippians 4:1-9
11	Ps.51:1-13	Mark 6:1-29	Philippians 4:10-23
12	Ps.63:1-5	Mark 6:30-56	Colossians 1:1-8
13	Ps.73:1-17	Mark 7:1-23	Colossians 1:9-14
14	Ps.73:21-28	Mark 7:24-37	Colossians 1:15-23
15	Ps.84	Mark 8:1-21	Colossians 1:24-2:5
16	Ps.95:1-7	Mark 8:22-9:1	Colossians 2:6-7
17	Ps.96:1-6	Mark 9:2-32	Colossians 2:8-23
18	Ps.100	Mark 9:33-50	Colossians 3:1-11
19	Ps.103:1-5	Mark 10:1-31	Colossians 3:12-17
20	Ps.103:6-14	Mark 10:32-52	Colossians 3:18-4:1
21	Ps.103:15-22	Mark 11:1-19	Colossians 4:2-6
22	Ps.108:1-5	Mark 11:20-33	Colossians 4:7-18
23	Ps.111	Mark 12:1-27	1Thess. 1:1-10
24	Ps.112	Mark 12:28-44	1Thess. 2:1-16
25	Ps.121	Mark 13:1-23	1Thess. 2:17-3:5
26	Ps.127	Mark 13:24-37	1Thess. 3:6-13
27	Ps.133:1	Mark 14:1-26	1Thess. 4:1-12
28	Ps.139:1-6	Mark 14:27-52	1Thess. 4:13-18
29	Ps.139:7-16	Mark 14-15:20	1Thess. 5:1-11
30	Ps.139:17-24	Mark 15:21-47	1Thess. 5:12-28
31	Ps.147:1-6	Mark 16:1-8